BAD GIRL

ISBN: 978-1-968970-17-8 Paperback
ISBN: 978-1-971940-30-4 Hardback
ISBN: 978-1-968970-16-1 Ebook

Rev. date: 02/24/2026

FAY E. B. DOWNING

BAD GIRL

Dedication

This book is dedicated first to God, who, through His grace, mercy, goodness and love, gave me the ability to write it. Second, to my precious Godmother, Carolyn Davis Downing. She is the one that stuck with me through thick and thin. She was a mother to the motherless. She never stopped praying for me.

Acknowledgment

To God be the glory! He is truly a wonder in my soul, the love of my life, and a guide to my pathway to heaven. God has been better to me than I have been to myself. He has opened doors that no man can close and closed doors that no man can open. There is something about the name of Jesus that sets my soul on fire. He is the reason why I live.

To Mother Louvenuia Flournoy, who has now gone home to be with the Lord. Thank you for seeing a diamond in the rough.

To Althea Woodson-Robinson, who disciplined me to be a mighty woman of God, you led by example, and I thank you.

To Pauline Patterson, thank you for planting a seed in my life. You saw something in me among all the muck, the mire, and the filth.

Special thanks to Pastor Hilda N. Montgomery, who has loved me, cared for me and been there for me. Thank you for your help in all the ways I cannot mention. Above all, thank you for being a Woman after God's own heart.

To the one person that has fed me with spiritual bread during the times in my life that I needed most, Rev. Dr. A.O. Foreman, Jr., thank you.

You are truly an anointed gift from God, and my prayer is that He will bless you beyond your expectations. May God bless you and your family and always be a hedge of protection around you.

About the Author

Bold, gifted, short, loud, humble, courageous, nervous, shy, motivated, multi-talented, quiet, determined. Optimistic, patient, and ambitious — That is who I am.

I am one in a million with a heart of pure gold and, above all, a warrior. I am not a sweet-talker or show-off. I am unapologetically true to myself in everything I do. My life has not been easy, but I never gave up.

Above all, I am a sinner saved by Grace.

Contents

Chapter One — The Early Years

My tiny hands would clench tightly to the wooden door as I let myself suffocate inside the broom closet. Sweat beads would roll down my face; I would force my eyes shut, hoping the darkness would make it all go away.

If only we could dodge reality by closing our eyes, I would never dare to open my eyes again!

I would see a man in a military uniform approaching me; his strong hands would squeeze every ounce of my naïve soul. I was only four when that happened, and it continued happening for a long time. I didn't know what it was, but I wanted it all to stop.

"No. No. No," my little heart would scream.

I was too naïve to know what was happening, but I didn't like it. I was too numb to say anything, but my body would involuntarily move to push the culprit away and run far, far away, to the fairyland I had heard about.

The darkness inside the closet, the military uniform, the feel of an unwelcoming touch, and the yearning to get past it; are some of the vivid childhood memories that are etched deep in my mind. I got chills down my spine for a long time whenever the flashbacks gushed in front of me.

It was one of the several incidents that shaped my personality. My life had been a bumpy ride since childhood, and I wonder what would have happened if God had not been by my side to shield me at every step.

My life journey began in Norfolk, Virginia, in the late 1950s; it was a seasonal change of reflection, and some mornings would be cool, but the days would be warm. It kind of sums up who I am — my personality, my life, and my path. I grew up in a dysfunctional family where my parents had so much on their plates that they never paid attention to me.

My mom and dad were both from underprivileged black families; they belonged to working-class families who struggled all their lives to make ends meet. My mother's family belonged to a farming community, and my father's family came from a fishing background on the Eastern shore of Virginia. My grandfather on my father's side was half-Indian. He wore his hair in plaits from the 1960s up until his death. I always remember my father saying. Don't forget you are half-Indian. Maybe not half, but maybe a fourth or an eighth. What plague the Indian culture is alcoholism, incest, and suicide. I guess I am one-fourth.

My father was the eldest son in a family of seven. Jackie was their aunt's son by my grandfather, but he was raised by my grandmother as her youngest son. My grandfather lived on Virginia's eastern shore; he would bring us fish whenever he visited us. My grandfather had three families, but all were scattered and distant.

There is no denying that my father had to put in a lot of effort from a very young age. He was only sixteen when he joined the military during World War II. He got into a fight with a white man (this was during the time of segregation). He was given two choices, go to jail or join the U.S. army. He enlisted in the army in 1944. His job was to handle the dead. I grew up listening to his experiences in Germany and seeing his black-and-white photos. I actually remember one picture of a big pile of dead soldiers.

My father left the army when World War II was over. He received automotive instruction, so he could work as a skilled mechanic.

On the other hand, my mom had eight members in her family, and she was the second child after Aunt Yvonne, the eldest. My mother was beautiful in all her essence. Yet, her beauty did not shield her from enduring the obstacles that life threw her way.

My mother was never employed nor experienced life outside of our home. She never experienced dining out, going to movie theatres, or having a family night because these things were non-existent. I believe rearing a dozen kids was enough labor for her. While my parents had their fair share of lack, one thing they were clearly not so good at was family planning. One of my mother's younger sisters wanted to rear me, but my mother and father were not in agreement. I guess they knew I would be needed to care for all the siblings that would come after me.

I was the fourth among eleven children; our giant family lived in a small house. Consequently, we moved frequently. My siblings and I would eat beans of all kinds most days while sitting around two tables. Some days, we didn't have any food. They would be the days when we would all sit inside on the steps and sing *Mama is a do-do head*, or *I'm hungry*. It was a time when people had large families, and my parents were no exception. However, the need to have a dozen kids is beyond my comprehension.

My father often worked two jobs simultaneously (to make provisions for his family during these difficult times) as it was difficult to provide for everyone. He would get paid every two weeks and purchase hotdogs and red beans. It was a tremendous treat for us because, during those times, we couldn't afford the luxury of eating a variety of foods/ or candies and cookies every other day.

From what I observed from their old photos, I could see that my mother was in love with my father. But my experiences taught me that love doesn't necessarily guarantee the happiness and fulfillment one craves in life.

My parents did not have a healthy relationship; my mother had to deal with certain accusations about my father that scarred her for life. Our family deteriorated with each passing day, and each of us had to go through various grief-stricken life stages from a very early age.

At the same time, I realized that the ups and downs of life are inevitable, and every family goes through them. However, it was constant for some people, while for others, it was temporary.

Growing up as a child, I had no say in the toxic family environment, so I endured continuous trauma and agony that emotionally scarred me for life.

The saddening trajectory that can occur for anyone at a very young age is being a victim of abuse and deprived of parental love. I suffered from both, not just once but on several occasions.

Sometimes I wonder if my parents had the happiest of marriages because there were a lot of fights, harassment, and blame. For a young mind, these incidents made me acquire a completely different perception of the term *parents*.

My earliest memory of myself is from when I was four. We were living in row houses at Carney Park, which was originally built for the military families returning home.

When it came to bringing people home, my dad was kind of strict and didn't allow just anyone to come inside. He had one friend, Mr. Booker T., whom he had met while serving in the military, and they remained friends for a while.

Booker T. was the only male my father permitted to enter the house; the two would often sit in the kitchen and drink. When Brooker T. would visit my father, he always wore his military uniform, and his very presence would bring me shivers; I would feel an unexplainable sense of uneasiness around him.

Booker T. would offer me candies and make me sit on his lap. I didn't realize that I was being sexually assaulted until I gained a sense of my surroundings twenty or thirty years later.

The episodes of shivering and paranoia when I hid in the closet haunt me to this day. I would quietly wait for Mr. Booker T. to leave with an ever-increasing heart rate and rapid breathing.

The house we lived in, in Norfolk, was not particularly big, but somehow, I would still manage to find a place to escape because his presence would frighten me to the core.

It remained a pattern for a long time, and I didn't have the strength to break it. Every time he visited, it would bring back memories of the assault and trigger my fear response.

I didn't understand how he managed to do it in front of my father, but he took some indecent liberties with me. He would tweak my then non-existent breast and touch me inappropriately at various parts of my body.

It must be what his lust desired, and he might have gained temporary pleasure, but the lifetime scar it left on me could never be healed. I had no one to blame, but I frequently regretted my parents' lack of awareness, and I want to say love and support as a child.

After this incident, everything frightened me. Undesirable situations would trigger anxiety within me within minutes. I felt miserable as the trauma wouldn't leave and had a long impact on my life.

Booker T. eventually ceased dropping by, but the damage was already done. I remember it was the only time I felt serene and content for the time being. Hence, the trauma and terror persisted.

I was a victim of sexual assault and emotional neglect, and I believe these experiences shaped my life from an early age. The experience did not only frame my sexuality but also taught me to stay out of everybody's way. The little girl in the closet believed she had to endure all the pain alone!

At a very young age, I learned that it was me, all by myself; it was me against the world. It was significant for me to consider my sentiments and pull myself out of that dark stage because, at the same time, I had no support from my family.

But no matter how I tried to get over it, the persistent emotions of shame, phobia, and guilt remained. I coped with these terrible feelings by keeping them a top secret. Along with the pain, I had to live with scars every day and craved parental love simultaneously. At times it would bring tears to my eyes and poignantly echo the trauma.

I wanted attention, and my naïve mind would carve out ways to get it. As one of my coping mechanisms, I would steal my brothers' milk bottles. My mother had children consistently, one year after another, and at that time, I had four brothers younger than me.

Stealing their milk bottle was a minor way to gain control over my meager life because it made me feel good and secure. I was taller than them and would easily retrieve their bottles from the crib or bassinet, making me feel superior.

Rolling my shirt while sucking on the milk bottles (which gave me a sense of satisfaction) until I too-quickly scampered off the crib, which was in the hallway, spraining my leg. After that, I could no longer retrieve them; I had to figure out another way to gain control.

I remember waiting until the babies were fully asleep. Then, I would quietly, slowly, and smoothly ease the bottle out of their lips. Later, I would hide under their crib and completely drink all of it, making sure to put it back quietly.

I didn't know what I was doing, but I felt good doing it as it was an attempt to get my parents' attention.

It also gave me a sense of achievement; just like most children, I repeated this pattern of behavior until I was caught. Even though I used to be right there in the middle of all the children, no one ever paid attention to me.

My parents never had time for me, and they never paid me any attention. I guess you could say my family was dysfunctional.

As a result, I perceived it as a source of amusement, but secretly, I craved parental attention. My mother even made sarcastic and nasty comments about me stealing my siblings' milk bottles decades later.

Sibling rivalry is common and does not always result in animosity. Yet, sibling relations could be destructive when compounded with other factors, such as a problematic familial environment and toxic relations between your parents. Similarly, my relationship with a handful of my siblings was neither healthy nor pleasant.

Up until I was six, we lived in the projects. My mom had two miscarriages before Giggs was born. He was the oldest of the siblings and was as quick as his name.

Giggs, being the oldest, was responsible for looking after his younger siblings and ensuring they ate breakfast. He was seven when he carried out his responsibilities of taking care of his siblings while attending school. His presence in the house was more like an authoritative spirit.

At seventeen, he graduated from high school and joined the U. S. Navy.

My older sister was Christine, and just like any other sibling rivalry, we also had a love-hate relationship. We all had nicknames, and Christine's nickname was Rusty. She didn't grow up with good, loving parents either; she also had to heal from deep wounds as my mother would abuse her and curse her. The relationship between Christine and my mother was so deeply entangled that the bond seemed irreparable. She lived a more wretched life while residing in the home than any of us.

The third sibling in the sequence was Paul; he would always consider himself in competition with Giggs, so he tried to be superior, the better one. He made efforts to get what Giggs had, which continued even after they grew up. Later, he enlisted in the military for a few years and became a policeman. Not long after he was kicked off the police force for allegedly stealing a boat, he moved to North Carolina, where he was employed as a mechanic at Camp LeJeune.

I believe Paul did everything right for himself after all the disturbance and conflicts he went through within the family. There were not many grandchildren as one would think, keeping in mind that my dad's line was really long with seven sons and four daughters, but still, none of my brothers had any boys and only one daughter.

Let's just say it because he said it; he did not like black women. Although Paul, nicknamed Tik-Top, married a white woman, he never had any kids of his own. Brenda had two or three kids, and while he was still married, he got with another white woman. On the other hand, I recall that he married a Croatian woman two years ago after falling in love with her online, but the marriage did not last long.

Even though my siblings' relationship found its root in family boundaries, Roger or Dee Dee and I were very close. It was always fascinating to be in his presence, and I admired him.

Unfortunately, Dee Dee got involved with drugs inspired by my dad's youngest brother, Heads. His name was Heads for a reason; he believed he could get over on everybody and anybody. As a theater and radio station manager, he created a singing group and published their first song, which had only one hit. Even that was a knockoff; I found out when I googled it.

However, illegal drug trafficking opened the doors of the prison for Roger. For a long time, it was believed that Roger committed suicide by hanging himself in prison. But, Paul, who always enjoyed putting a beautiful spin on everything, asserted that Roger suffered an attack and the guards were trying to restrain him while he passed away.

Roger was young when he died compared to Donald, who was a beautiful boy, but his life was miserable and meant nothing to him. He went into the army for less than six months. He would drink excessively, and it appeared that his neurological system had the capacity for him to consume small amounts of alcohol and become euphoric. Later, he fell and seriously injured his head fatally, dying a mournful death.

Another of my brothers was Robert, nicknamed Slim, yet we called him Bernard. He was a very skinny, smart and beautiful child. He joined the Navy also and later worked as a mechanic at Nautilus. He was off to a good start.

Like Donald, Bernard also had an atrocious habit of overindulging in alcoholic beverages. However, I was unaware that he was homosexual until he gave me his red pair of shoes. My sister Twinkie shared this with me. That was before everybody was "coming out of the closet" and disclosing their homosexual tendencies. While Bernard was in the service, he dated a woman who looked more like a man than a female but never married. Later, he was diagnosed with AIDS, which became one of the causes of his death in a nursing home.

Then, there was Clarence, who became addicted to drugs and alcohol. However, it feels pleasant to say that he got his life together for the most part. He has a good job at a machinery shop and later bought a home. I was immensely proud of him when he quit smoking, drinking, and doing drugs. It felt good to see my younger brother doing well for himself.

My mother had another baby between Clarence and my sister, Twinkie, but unfortunately, this child would not live long, dying of crib death one or two months after his birth.

Twinkie was nine years younger than me and was close to my heart. I loved her, and I remember holding her in my arms when we moved to Villa Circle. Despite suffering from the brunt of Mama calling her all kinds of rude and disgusting names, Twinkie got her life together as she is a very intelligent and sharp-witted businesswoman. I am proud of her, but she had her problems, too.

Another of my brothers was Jeffery, and his nickname was Bop. I had a wonderful relationship with him, characterized by love and compassion. When he was a baby, I accidentally dropped him on the concrete floor; he was rendered unconscious and got a concussion, but fortunately, he had a miraculous recovery.

Bop attended school; he saw his siblings stuck in a loop of nothing. It seemed too hard for him, and it appeared as if he no longer wanted to keep playing a role in the tragedy of errors. He was unable to discover a purpose for his existence, so later on, on the date he turned 21, he committed suicide.

The youngest of my siblings was "Stump." She was married twice, and her life was truly affected by the familial environment, just like most of us. After talking to her, I must admit that she suffered almost as much as Christine did. Out of all of us, she took after Mom and had six children. It was not easy for her to engage in beneficial developmental activities due to several factors, including instability in the home environment.

As we all came from a family where we lacked love and attention, it was difficult to evaluate the impact it had on our lives. Some of us overcame the traumas and miseries and got our lives together, but at the same time, it was not easy to grow up and come from such a deep level of dysfunction. Although misery and helplessness still exist today, things have begun to come together by the grace of God.

We, the siblings, were distant and had complicated relationships, but I sometimes believe some paths have led us closer to each other. However, in my family, there were no roads but just underground tunnels. I believe my siblings and I found ourselves lost in that tunnel, but we learned in our own way how to survive there.

From an early age, I was exposed to the darkness and cruelties of the world; I spent most of my life searching for love, gentleness, and peace. Everything I grew up watching and experiencing had adversely affected my personality and shaped my future and my relationship with my siblings.

Chapter Two — Seven to Nine-Years-Old Dynamics of My Highly Dysfunctional Family

"See, I think there are roads that lead us to each other. But in my family, there were no roads — just underground tunnels. I think we all got lost in those underground tunnels. No, not lost. We just lived there."

— Benjamin Alire Sáenz

They say the relationship between parents directly affects children; it lays the foundation of their personality, life choices, and overall behavior. It determines the course of life they would embark on and impacts the important decisions shaping their lives. I strongly believe it to be true as I endured the trauma of growing up in a dysfunctional family since I developed an understanding of meaningful relationships.

It's not like my mother and father never loved each other; whenever I looked at old photos of their early married life, I thought they were so in love. My mother was the epitome of beauty, and my father, on the other hand, looked handsome in his military uniform. They started their family with big dreams, being in love — whatever the word love meant for them at that time. It's the law of life; it doesn't spare anyone. Cruelties of life come in all forms, shapes, and sizes; sometimes, they leave a scar on a person's mind that can never be healed. We all come into this world with a fair share of ups and downs but do not all possess the same strength to deal with hardships the same way, and it ends up leaving a huge impact on our lives and the quality of the decisions we make.

My parents were no different; together, they made a gorgeous couple, but even they could not save their relationship from getting affected when things went downhill. Their love began to fade until nothing was left other than bitterness.

We lived on the borderline of poverty. I grew up watching my father work all the time outside while my mother took care of the children at home. Perhaps, things could have been different financially if my mother had worked too, but then, there would be no one to watch the kids. It was not common for women to work outside in that era; just like other women, my mother was a homemaker, and I never blamed her for that.

While we evidently lacked financial security, the emotional negligence, sexual assault, and abuse that I witnessed at a young age further drowned me deep into the ocean of darkness.

As a child, I remember seeing my father hug my mother a few times, but that's all. They never showed affection toward each other, at least in front of the children. Not to mention, they never showed us any outward affection at all. However, they did not stop fighting or abusing each other in our presence. Our family environment was not exactly loving, so we never learned to love ourselves, let alone others.

Maybe all relationships start as bitter-sweet, and it takes constant efforts and affection to keep the sweetness alive; otherwise, the love fades away, leaving a void that is hard to fulfill.

I was too young to understand the meaning of *infidelity* when I was exposed to it. It was yet another thing that further derailed us from living a happy life as a family, as my parents started fighting more often.

It all started when my father started spending more time with my aunt Yvonne. She was my mom's sister, the eldest among the siblings. They were both very attractive women. During childhood, my aunt Yvonne would often visit us. She was married and had ten kids; however, not all of them were fathered by her husband.

As far as I remember, six of her kids were from her husband, while the youngest four were from different men she saw at different times. It was no secret to anyone, and as a child, I never found anything wrong with it either.

Aunt Yvonne was the kind of a woman who would have men around her all the time. She liked to party; she often invited my father to her place, where they would hang out. There would be other people, and whenever they would hang out with one another, they would be flirting and joking constantly.

I believe Aunt Yvonne was in love with my dad. Maybe because she found him first, but eventually, my dad became attracted to my mom, and they got married. My mother would often say, "Aunt Yvonne loves men." But I think it was because she loved them too.

Later, Aunt Yvonne stopped visiting us as much as she used to. It was not negligence on her side, but maybe her routine was like that; she mostly had time at night. Nonetheless, the troubles at our place more or less remained the same.

My mom stayed married to my dad, and they had a lot of kids together. Their relationship started deteriorating, be it because of financial constraints, declining social status, or other problems. Perhaps, it was due to the pressure of day-to-day living life and earning for a big family that my dad started drinking more and more. Especially on Fridays, whenever he would come home, he would be drunk. We could tell that he was high then; he would smell like alcohol all the time.

Our father always remained distant from us. I wonder how life would have been if we were close to him growing up. *Would he be able to understand our troubles regardless of how vague they seem? Did he have the patience to treat all eleven children with love and kindness?* I guess I will never know.

I hardly recall having any interaction with my father around this age. I don't think that we talked much as he was mostly away for work, and whenever he would be back home on the weekends, he would be drinking or drunk.

Whenever he would return home drunk, he would abuse my mother and demand to have sex. Whether they had a healthy physical relationship or not, they did have a lot of sex. After all, they had so many children together.

Out of nowhere, I remember my mother coming back with another baby in her arms one day. It had not been long since she had arrived with a new baby when she got into a huge fight with my father, which led her to stab him in the end. I remember the stabbing because it was so close to his heart; just a few more inches, and that would have been it.

Since my childhood, I have seen them fighting over money and the debate of what's wrong and what's right. But it was neither of these things this time. The fight erupted when my father came home drunk and wanted to have sex. However, my mom refused, and they started arguing. Things got worse to such an extent he hit her on her head. It was not the first time my dad hit my mom, as physical and verbal abuse was common in our house.

That particular day, he must have abused her that time, and things escalated quickly, and they indulged in a physical fight. I remember he was lying on his sofa in the dining room because he was very drunk when my mom's refusal made him angry. Before my mother stabbed him, she threw boiling hot water on my father.

Due to these never-ending fights, we, the children, could never experience what it felt like to be loved and cared for. Each of us was going through a different phase of life, and just like most children, we also felt lost and had so many questions. We didn't grow up in a culture where openness was encouraged; we would fear and hesitate to share anything with our parents as we didn't want to add more problems to their already troubled life. We could not tell them what we liked and didn't like and accepted everything they provided, regardless of how big or small it was.

We all slept in two sets of bunk beds. There was a black-and-white TV, and all of us would sit in such a manner that everyone could see it. We would watch whatever shows aired then, and it was perhaps the only source of entertainment other than playing with each other.

Whenever our parents would fight, we would get so scared that we all would wet in bed. They would scream at the top of their lungs, and we covered our ears with our hands to avoid listening to anything that could further make us anxious. We had diapers made up of sheets back then, and every time one of us wet in bed, we had to hang the diapers and the sheets out to dry the next morning. We all experienced bedwetting, especially my brothers Paul, Fats, Slim, and Roger, and they also sucked their thumbs as they felt insecure and anxious.

My mind and body began experiencing changes as I entered my early teens. I quit wetting the bed when I turned 12 and started my period. I only wore one pair of underwear to school. I would wash my underwear and hang it out to dry every night. This was when we moved from the projects to the two-story house. So, I would hang my underwear on the banner or the railing of the stairs. I was not the only one, and all my siblings more or less survived living in the same manner.

Finally, the good time came, but it was not all good. We now had enough rooms to cater to our large family. I shared my room with my sister, and all the boys shared a room. My mom and dad got a separate room for themselves.

It was a two-story house with three bedrooms. I remember climbing up and down the staircase leading to the living room. There was a couch in the dining room where we would sit to watch TV. On one side, there was the kitchen leading out toward the hallway.

My mom mostly spent her time downstairs cooking supper in the kitchen or watching television or both. There would often be a pot of beans and some homemade biscuits. To keep her distracted from all the troubling things, she would read romance magazine stories all day. That was her way of coping with whatever she was going through in her married life with my father. She had no option but to cope because she could not run back to her dad's house as there was no one to look after her or the kids. Unfortunately, my grandmother also died when I was a baby; she was the kind of person who would make the best out of a bad situation. She was young when she died.

There would be days when we would all sit inside on the steps and sing, *Mama is a do-do head*, or *I'm hungry*. It didn't faze my mom at all; we would eat when she deemed it was time to eat. There would be oatmeal and homemade biscuits; I would struggle to finish my oatmeal. The two-story house had a backyard with fruit trees; one of our neighbors had a grapevine, the other had a pear tree, and we had peach trees. It felt great every time we would get to eat fruit that would fall in our backyard. At that time, we did not get food stamps or dried food from the government, so we had to live with whatever we had.

We didn't have a washing machine, and we used to hang clothes out on the clothesline. We would hang out our diapers and sheets to dry out as well. When we moved out of the two-story house, we started getting cheese and powdered milk from the government. Things eventually started to settle down, and life was headed in the right direction. We were not as hungry as we always had been. We all still remained pretty thin but never had to go to the doctor.

The only time Dad took us all in a car to the doctor was when we all fell mildly sick with a bad rash. However, we discovered that it was due to the detergent we used to wash our clothes. Otherwise, we never went to the doctor as we never got sick.

My dad did multiple jobs, but at the same time, whatever he earned was not spent wisely. They mismanaged the money, and we could not ever save a penny. My father would not bring all of his pay check home, leading to an argument between him and my mom. He would spend money on drinking, and we would have no money to pay the rent. Sometimes there would be no lights; sometimes, we would survive without water; sometimes, we slept without eating anything. No one knew if he even made enough money to support all of the kids. However, our financial problems got worse due to my dad's drinking problem.

That's how I grew up, and now that I think about it, I'm glad my child did not have to endure the same troubles I experienced while growing up.

We didn't have a beautiful house, nor was our house full of beautiful furniture and other luxuries. But it didn't matter because, since childhood, we were never exposed to a luxurious life; we started seeing troubles as a part of life that we had to endure whether we liked it or not.

I guess that's what life is; it keeps going on.

Chapter Three — Wild Times 9 to 14

The Beginning of the End — The Incest Between My Dad and Oldest Sister

"Unhappiness in a child accumulates because he sees no end to the dark tunnel. The thirteen weeks of a term might just as well be thirteen years."

— Graeme Greene

"Why is this happening to me and not to you?"

To this day, Christine's voice echoes in my head. My heart still aches for the pain she endured alone. I wish I was old enough to stop it from happening and strong enough to protect her. *But who was I to protect her from?* The people we called our parents? The same people who were meant to protect us and whom we trusted the most.

My heart swells with love when I see a herd of elephants circling around their youngest ones as they walk from one destination to another. When I see a litter of stray cats or dogs where the mother feeds, cleans, and protects the little ones all alone, risking her own life, it is fascinating how a mother, regardless of the species, is always there to shield her kids until they are old enough to protect themselves. This is what makes motherhood the noblest of all relations; this is what mothers are remembered for — their selfless love for their children.

But what about the people who are deprived of this blessing? Or those who are betrayed and exploited by their own? The children who get no protection from the cruelties of the world and their naïve hearts cannot even trust those who brought them into this world. Whether situational or circumstantial, the negligence and abuse a child faces at the hands of their parents can drastically impact their personality and cause irreparable damage.

My older sister Christine was one such victim, and my heart still aches for all the things she went through — before and after our lives changed forever.

It all started when my dad started drinking more than ever. Though he had a very good job at the Naval Base at that time, whenever he would return home each night, he would get drunk and out of his senses. During this period, he always worked and then drank. He was a functioning alcoholic. I was only 10 or 11 at that time, struggling to develop an understanding of the family dynamics and the issues that persisted within our home.

Christine was 15 when it happened. I wonder if she even knew what was happening or what pressured her to cave in. I don't exactly know when it happened or how many times it happened, but our father had sexual intercourse with my older sister – his own and oldest daughter.

The entire world collapsed; our lives turned upside down. It was the beginning of the end.

I was too young to understand the gravity of the situation and how the incest between my father and my sister was going to scar all of our lives forever. A scar that can never be healed.

When my mother found out, it wreaked havoc at our house. That was the day when she transformed into a whole new person who was unrecognizable by her own kids. It was the final nail in the coffin of her already withering relationship with my father. The trauma that followed affected all of us.

It happened when our family was living in the upstairs apartment and the basement of a big old house. My dad had cut a hole in the floor and created a space to put some steps so the kids wouldn't have to go outside to go to the basement. The image of the basement is still vivid in my head. Even though we had electricity, water, and some heat, it was dark — very dark.

My dad would take Christine to the basement in one of the dark rooms down there. The worst part of it all was that even though he was sorry for what happened, he never realized the gravity of what he had done and how it was going to ruin our family. It was not a one-time mistake, nor did it happen by accident. I remember when he had tried to get into my bed too, but I was quick to jump out of it right away. I was a little girl then, but I knew it wasn't right, and my reflexes saved me from going through what my sister had to face alone.

Christine was four years older than me, and just like every little girl, I would often look up to her. I had light brown skin, while hers was dark brown; although it made no difference to me, it did bother her, and perhaps, she developed an insecurity that only became obvious after this incident. As children, we never cursed at each other or had any fights or even disagreements up until this point. It was like everything had been affected, be it as little as having meals together or the fact that all of us suffered from emotional neglect and abuse. Everything was falling apart.

While we, the children, were struggling to cope in our own ways, my mother was absolutely devastated. She called the police and involved child protective services as well. However, since Christine never gave the exact dates, my mom was told to make up the dates on her own. I still don't know the reason why neither my mother nor Christine couldn't or wouldn't come up with the dates, but it made matters worse further ahead. The system wasn't as efficient as it is today, and since the actual dates of the incidences were never provided, in the eyes of the authorities, it never happened.

Instead of letting the police deal with it, my mother decided to take matters into her own hands. It was the worst decision she made as a mother and, to be honest, as a person. It is when she unleashed her wrath on Christine, the victim herself. I called this the period of blaming the victim.

It was around the time when my mother's drinking had worsened, and the decisions she made following this incident still send shivers down my spine. She became a monster, while my dad turned into a zombie that only drank.

I couldn't understand why she developed a grudge against Christine and took all her anger, frustration, and scorn out on her. She was agonized about being betrayed by the man she married and had all those children with. I understand she was hurt, but it didn't justify her unimaginable and unspeakable treatment of her own daughter.

My mother had Christine march around naked in the house in front of everyone. My heart aches to even imagine the pain, embarrassment, and trauma a teenage girl must have gone through to walk naked in front of her younger siblings. I don't even remember how long it went on till my mother finally gave her a sheet to wrap around herself. Before this incident, Christine and I shared one of the bedrooms; however, later, Christine was relegated to the cellar, where she lived, ate, and survived for the next two or three months. It seemed like years.

I remember how we all felt sorry for Christine; my older brother Giggs wanted to protect her, but even he couldn't make it stop. All of Christine's hair had fallen out because of stress and anxiety. My mother cursed her and verbally, if not physically, abused her. Being a minor, Christine was evidently a victim in this case, while my father was the culprit. My mother only turned her life into a living hell and did not let go of any chance to shame her in front of us all.

"You are a whore. A tramp. A strumpet!"

She would scream at the top of her lungs every time she would see Christine. My mother then isolated herself in her room; she would sleep all day with the door closed, get up at night, and drink most of the time. The situations were only getting uglier with time; everything was falling apart, and there was no one to hold us together.

My father was kicked out of the bedroom by my mother, and he was asked to leave the house during the Christmas holidays. However, he was only gone for a few days. My mother had transformed into a whole new person, and her cold-heartedness had made survival unbearable at home. Christine was angry, ashamed, and agonized. The poor girl didn't even get the chance to share her trauma and get her feelings acknowledged by her mother. I wonder if things would have been different if my mother had listened to her instead of blaming her for everything that happened. I wonder how our lives might have been different if we had not endured the betrayal, pain, and trauma at the hands of our own parents.

"You are Mama's favorite!"

I still don't understand why Christine was mad at me because I never did anything to hurt her or make her feel any less. Perhaps, she wanted me to show more compassion toward her, which I was unable to do, being a clueless child myself. If only I knew how to console a traumatized child and a victim of sexual and emotional abuse, I might have been a better sister to her.

I don't know why she assumed it, but I was no one's favorite, and as far as I remember, my mother didn't favor me in any way. I had my own share of struggles, just like the rest of my siblings. I wonder what I could have done to make her trust that I was on her side. I never blamed her; after what I had witnessed her go through, I could never blame her.

Not just me, Christine was mad at everyone, and things only worsened at home with time. When my brother Giggs finally joined the Navy. He returned home and arranged for Christine to live with his girlfriend's family for a while till she could figure out her own way out.

After Christine moved out and Giggs left for his job, the responsibility of preparing meals and making sure everyone went to school and had lunch and dinner to eat fell on me. I managed the house chores, filled the role of a parent figure for my siblings, and still managed to get good grades in school. As I sit back now and reminisce over the memories, I realize that I got good grades and became a good student because of the attention paid to me by my teachers and the immense amount of attention I paid to my coursework. They praised me and thought I was a good girl, something my parents never told me. It was my way of escaping and coping with the negligence I endured as a child; it was my salvation.

Christine hated me, she hated Mama, and she hated everyone else. I don't condone hate, but I have always tried to understand what made her feel that way. We never had a close relationship. I tried, but maybe I didn't try hard enough. She decided to take charge of her life and live where she wasn't judged, abused, or assaulted. Within a year after she moved out of the house, she had a kid and another one after a few years. I do not know if her first child was a result of incest. I do know that her child and, later, her grandchild wanted nothing to do with the family. *Can you blame them?* Throughout her life, she had severe health problems, and she suffered a lot.

Despite it all, she never returned home.

Chapter Four — The Boston Exodus

At the start of any relationship, our eyes tend to seek happiness amidst all the uncertainties. However, when it ends, even the recollection of pleasant memories stabs our souls and makes us question our choices. *Was it all worth it?* I guess the wounds never heal, and no matter how much we try, the pain and trauma return to haunt us in one way or another.

After staying in an abusive marriage for many years, resulting in physical, emotional, and mental turmoil, my mom finally decided to leave my dad. I believe my mother's side of the family, including her brothers and sisters, was aware of what happened between my dad and my sister Christine. They knew that my mom suffered physical and verbal abuse at my father's hands and everything else that was going on in our house. Finally, my maternal aunts and uncles got together and arranged some money for my mother to go to Boston, where her oldest sister was living. That was the beginning of our exodus to Boston!

By this time, my mother had ten children; however, not of all of them were living together. Two of my older siblings had moved out while my mother prepared to leave for Boston with the remaining eight.

As children, we all got very excited about this trip. We didn't know what was going on but took it as an adventure. It was the first time we traveled on a bus, and we had to walk to the bus station about two miles from home. After we reached the bus station, we boarded the Greyhound bus. Being the eldest of the siblings, my brother Paul made sure that every one of us had water and something to eat.

Since we had never traveled by bus before, it was a new experience for all of us — more like an adventure.

When we arrived in Boston, the weather was cold and snowy. I don't remember exactly, but it took us about twelve hours to reach our new destination. Finally, we arrived at Aunt Yvonne's apartment, where she lived with her six children. It was a small apartment, but since we had no other place to go, we stayed there for the time being while my mother searched for a new place.

My mother was pregnant before we left Norfolk, and she gave birth to a baby in Boston. However, the baby had a hole in its heart and couldn't survive. My mother had taken a big step when she decided to leave the man she was married to and the house where she was raising her children. After everything she faced, especially during the last few years, she needed time to move past the traumatic events that made her bitter and cold toward her own children. When we started living at Aunt Yvonne's house, my mother knew that we were safe, and she began to feel normal again.

This period brought much-needed calmness to our otherwise chaotic lives. Even if it was for a little while, we felt secure and safe while living at Aunt Yvonne's place. I remember my mother and Aunt Yvonne would party in the apartment and have men over. Seeing my mother happy and smiling after a long time was a relief. Aunt Yvonne's apartment was not spacious; it would get overcrowded whenever they hosted a party. Whenever there was a party in the house, my cousin Brenda and I would have our own little party upstairs. That's when I drank wine for the first time. I started drinking Boones Farm, and I thought it tasted fantastic.

I was a teenager at the time. At this point in life, I started experiencing different emotions, and my eyes were set on exploring new things and embarking on new adventures.

The fact that there was no one watching over me made me feel free. I liked a few boys, but I didn't do anything about it.

Soon afterward, we moved out of Aunt Yvonne's apartment after my mother found a new place. It was our first apartment in Boston, and the feeling of having our own home was comforting. I remember the weather in Boston was so cold. that we would have ice inside the windows. The apartment we moved into later on was bigger. It appeared as if big houses had been cut up into apartments to accommodate more families. Even though the weather was cold, it was a nicer place to live compared to where we came from in Norfolk, Virginia. It was a relief not to stress about the life we left, even though the weather was awful there. For the first time in a long time, I was happy. I was free. Even if it was only for a little while.

However, we lived there for a little while before my mother found a furnished apartment. I remember she had bought bunk beds for the children as she was getting welfare assistance from the government. Thanks to all the food stamps, we had good food on our table at last.

I was growing up, and at that time, I considered it a relief that no one was watching over me. I was enrolled in a school located at the top of the hill. I remember the path that went straight down the slope leading to our house. However, since the hill would be covered in ice and snow, it would be difficult to go down.

One day, I lost my way back from school. It was perhaps one of the first few days of school; I was new to the neighborhood and didn't know my way around. I only knew that our house was down Blue Hill Avenue, and I decided to go down that hill. However, my plan didn't succeed as I fell hard and bruised myself rolling down the icy slope. It was one of the worst experiences, and it left me bruised for a long time. I have a scar on my forehead to this day as a reminder.

It was an accident; I was just a child who lost her way home and stumbled on her way back. However, my family thought that I had gone crazy, which was one reason Mama considered going back home. "Fay has gone crazy," she would say. I think she was majoring on the minor at this point.

But was I really crazy? Or did I just need someone to hold my hand, comfort me, or maybe watch over me? I knew I craved attention, and I knew I wanted someone to guide me. Maybe that was why I would always find myself in trouble, even when I was just trying to be a good kid.

My oldest cousin Anne lived in the same building as us with her husband; our apartment was underneath theirs. I would often babysit their child, and her husband would walk me back to our apartment whenever she would return home. This was when he started taking advantage of me. As a teenager, I liked the attention he lavished on me, making me feel good about myself. However, I was still a virgin. I might have been bruised and abused, but I was still a virgin. Although we never had sex, I remember we got intimate. It made me happy at that moment, but only after I grew up did I realize how bad it was. When my cousin Anne found out what I had done, she stopped talking to me and cut contact with the entire family. Even after she divorced her husband, moved on, and got married again, she did not speak to me. This whole incident broke me and affected my ego as a child. Growing up, I realized I had hurt her and ruined her relationship with her husband, and she had every right to be mad at me.

While I was confused, scared, and ashamed of what had happened and trying to figure out how to make up for it, my mother blamed me entirely. Her anger was partially due to what happened between my father and Christine. My mother had still not gotten over the trauma of being betrayed, and her words depicted the mental turmoil she was going through. Her words were painful and echoed in my ears for a long time.

"You are just an over-sexed tramp! You are just like your older sister!"

We only stayed in Boston for four to five months, probably until spring. Around the same time, my dad sent a letter to Mom as he knew where we were living. It was a love letter in which he professed his love for her and how he had changed. He had also invited us to dinner. I only came across that letter after many decades, and I couldn't believe it when I read it. Every word in that letter depicted the most terrible phase we had experienced in our lives.

My father regretted his mistakes and choices, while my mother was finding it difficult to look after eight children on her own in a new place. My mother never told me about the letter, and I don't know what was going on in her mind when she received it. However, she told my older brother Paul that it was better for her to move back because she figured no one wanted to be with a woman with eight kids. Although she had tried to be strong when she ultimately made the tough decision of moving out, she gave up under ever-worsening circumstances and returned home to live with my father.

Once again, we got on the bus from Boston that was going to take us back to Virginia. When we arrived, my dad was there to pick us up. I believe something was wrong with his car that day because we had to walk back home from the bus station.

We walked on the same path and covered the same distance. However, this time we were coming back to what we had left. After we arrived home, I noticed that my dad had made a few changes around the place and also done a little cleaning.

Things remained good for a few days before it started going downhill again. My dad started drinking more than ever, while my mom had more children. As the boys grew up, they resisted and started fighting Dad. Whenever my older brother Paul would fight Dad, it would get ugly.

As if there weren't enough disturbances in our already chaotic lives, the remainder of our happiness crumbled into pieces bit by bit.

I wondered, "Did anything really change?" With time I believe, our lives only got worse.

Chapter Five — School Days

Memories are often evoked by little things — a fragrance that reminds us of sweet times, a melody that tugs at our heartstrings, or the sight of children filled with innocence who remind us of our carefree days.

As I sit here and recall the days of my school life, the memories are a blur, but the emotions are still strong and vivid enough to leave me nostalgic. To me, my school life was an escape from the terrible things that were going on in our family — at our home where I was supposed to feel safe and loved, but unfortunately, that was not the case. Amidst all the madness, confusion, and anger, I found comfort and solace outside the home each time I got acknowledged for who I really was as a child, as a student, and above all, as a young girl with big aspirations.

I went to an all-black school in our neighborhood which mostly comprised a black population. It was an elementary school through grades one to four; we didn't go to kindergarten. I remember how excited I would get to go to school every day. I was eager to learn; I wasn't into boys or any other thing at that time. My teachers would remain a major part of the memories of my school days. For a child like me who had witnessed all sorts of terrible things at home, it was a fascinating experience to learn exciting things about this world. I was eager to learn and expand my wings; my teachers helped me do that. I believe it was because of their efforts, acknowledgment, and appreciation that I became a better person. They helped me develop confidence in myself and encouraged my interest in education. I fondly remember Mrs. Rhodes; she was my second-grade teacher.

Every time I would do something, she would appreciate my efforts, and her words encouraged me to do better. I thank every one of my teachers as they awoke something in me — it was a thrill to learn new things.

We used to recite the Pledge of Allegiance at school at prayer time. It brought us the much-needed devotion that was missing in my life and made a huge difference.

Initially, I was enrolled in Titus Town Elementary School. It was also an all-black school, as this was during the time of segregation. I was a good student, better than average. I was always enthusiastic about learning new things each day and always got good grades. However, some of me always felt that I didn't click with the other girls in the class. Perhaps, that was the reason why I never had many friends. I studied fifth and sixth grade at Lindenwood Elementary School. At Lindenwood, the principal of the school was a distant relative from my father's side. I do not remember exactly, but I believe she was married to one of my great-uncles. However, segregation was prevalent not only in our society but also within our families. The principal didn't want to have anything to do with us because she thought we were from the wrong side of the tracks. Let's just say she didn't acknowledge us; it was like our presence never mattered to her or made any difference.

My brother Paul failed in the fifth grade and was in the same class as me. The only thing I remember vividly from that time is that I got myself into trouble for a silly comment I made to tease my classmate.

Back then, we didn't have social media or any gadgets. As children, we still found a way to express and share our thoughts with each other via slang books. These slang books were immensely popular among kids at that time. Whatever one student wrote in the slang book would go around from person to person as people would write things about different people. It was the 'cool thing' that kids loved to do and made snarky remarks about one another.

I did the same thing, not knowing that it would get me into trouble. In fifth grade, I commented in the slang book, "Robert Hall's mama is ugly." I still don't know why I said it, but the boy was going to whip my butt.

Thankfully, my brother Paul came to save me that day, and I never felt happier to have him in the same class.

In the fifth grade, I adored Mrs. Johnson. She was a black woman, a very good teacher, and an even greater human being. I believe it was she who awoke my spirit to learn more.

Around this time, I developed a new passion for reading books. Whether soap operas or romantic novels, weekly magazines, or the pornography my father brought, I started reading all types of books. Moreover, my paternal grandmother had a book service, and she would get us all types of arts and crafts books and other children's books. We had books of poems and riddles, fairy tales, to science. It was a cornucopia of books. I loved them all!

My passion turned me into an avid reader, and I would just read everything that I could get my hands on. Maybe it was the reason why I learned so much stuff that I shouldn't have learned at that age. I became more aware of myself at the age where my focus should have been different. The experience made me think and feel differently and piqued my interest in the opposite gender more than ever.

"Boys!" It would not be incorrect to say that they were the biggest highlight of my school life. Since elementary school, I never had girlfriends, and I was just crazy for the boys. *Sex* — it was all I could think of the entire time. I believe the reason why I always thought about boys and sex was that I never really got attention at home, and it was

the only way I thought I could feel loved. I was obviously wrong, but too young to understand it all then.

When I got into seventh grade, I wasn't dating any boy, and as far as I remember, no boy ever came to the house at that time. However, there was this guy named Tommy; he was my first boyfriend — that's how I like to remember him. Tommy and I would kiss each other in secluded areas in school and could never keep our hands off each other. The two of us never had sex, but we came very close. We loved to play in each other's arms and feel each other's bodies. Tommy thought he had taken my virginity, but I realized later that he did not know what he was doing. Regardless of that, I loved spending time with him.

As a young girl in her early teens, it made me believe that I was not missing out on anything and that *life was not that bad after all!*

As my eldest brother Giggs was in the Navy at that time, he had left some of his clothes at home. I loved dressing up as a boy, and whenever I got my hands on Gigg's clothes, I would wear them. We were poor, didn't have money to buy new clothes, and wore whatever we got our hands on, whether hand-me-downs or second-hand.

I remember I had a little wraparound skirt that I used to wear very often. When I first got my period in school, I was wearing the same skirt, and it ended up having a huge blood stain on the back. I was mortified that day; it was the most embarrassing moment of my school life. If only I had a little confidence in myself and a bit of awareness, I might have felt differently.

As years passed, I gradually developed into a different person, but nothing changed about my interests.

The middle school I attended, J. Cox Junior High School, was two miles from my home. My brother and I used to walk to school with other students from the neighborhood.

This experience gave me a chance to spend more time with the boys I liked in my area. I would get excited and look forward to spending more time with them every day.

I loved my school life, and I was intrigued each time I got to learn something new. However, what I didn't like about school was that the students would always be on the lookout to bully the odd one out.

My first rooting for the underdog was for two kids, Alfred, a Mongoloid kid, and the other guy Quinton Martin a tall and goofy-looking guy. They were among the kids who used to get bullied because they were different, and I used to feel bad for them because I knew I was different too. If not on the outside, definitely on the inside. I was damaged.

Only after I grew up did I realize I liked those guys because they were the underdogs in school. It was not like I wanted to go to bed with them or anything like that, but I liked them because they were being picked on, and I guess I could identify with them. Even though I wasn't bullied or picked on in school, I didn't fit in. Maybe, that's why I was different from the rest.

I went to Norview Junior High in the ninth grade after the Boston Exodus. It was a white-integrated school, and we had to ride on the bus because it was located far away from our home, approximately five miles.

My brother Paul and I would get one book of bus tickets which contained 20 tickets. We needed a bus ticket to go to and come from school. Each book would be divided between us and would last for two weeks. There were times when we didn't have money for the bus tickets and would have no other choice but to walk to and from school. It was terrible, but back then, we didn't have any other way to go to school, and I was definitely going to school to escape.

At Norview, seeing so many white people at the school was amazing, and it was a completely different experience for me. I got to meet and interact with different people while I was in the process of learning more about myself. I remember myself being a shy mouse back then among so many white little people.

In high school, I managed to get good grades, but in light of my previous academic progress, they were not great. My main focus was still on boys; for some reason, I didn't like white guys and was still more into black guys. Growing up, I would find myself thinking about the guys in my neighborhood all the time.

Around this time, I had a boyfriend, and although I never went out on any date, the two of us would spend time with each other at his place. I liked to call it an *extracurricular indoor activity*. To say that I was being promiscuous would have been an understatement.

I used to skip school to have sex with him because he lived not too far from the school. I used to skip classes to be with him; we would smoke and have sex. Because of this, my tenth-grade scores suffered quite a bit.

But I was in love — whatever love meant for me at that age. James Parker, aka Jimmy, was my first love, and I guess I will never forget the time I spent with him. I had started looking for love in all the wrong places because that's what I craved — love, affection, and attention.

I never really had a fatherly figure in my life that portrayed strength and love. My biological father was an alcoholic, unhappy and depressed, and haunted by demons, and because of everything that was going on at my house, I would always be on the lookout to find comfort in strangers.

At that time, Jimmy was my getaway. However, my heart shattered into pieces when he dumped me for a white girl in the eleventh grade. I hated him for that, and it took me a long time to get over it.

My thought process was messed up, and I never liked mixed couples. For me, it was somehow acceptable to see a black girl with a white guy but not the other way around. I was young and naïve, still developing an understanding of the world I lived in. It took me a long time to get over that because I hated it. It bothered me to see Jimmy with that white girl because of the same reason. Although Jimmy did want us to get back together later on, I had other things on my mind by then.

When I started going to Granby High School, I found out that it was also an integrated school. It must have been about three miles away from our home, and we used to walk to and from the school because we didn't have money for bus tickets.

In the eleventh grade, I started working after school and on the weekends. It was yet another way for me to escape the madness hovering over at our house. It was a pity; at that time, the only thing I did was have sex and smoke dope. That was ridiculous, and I was aware of it, but I couldn't do anything about it. My school life was mostly about studies and boys; I wasn't into sports or any other extracurricular activities. In twelfth grade, I joined FBLA (Future Business Leaders of America) and landed a $500 scholarship at Norfolk State University. It was a great achievement for me, but life had other plans.

I was unable to join Norfolk State University because, at the end of my senior year, I was pregnant. I knew that motherhood would significantly change my life, and at that time, I was not thinking about college even though I had excellent grades.

After having my child, circumstances changed drastically for me. However, my passion for studying further was still there, and finally, I decided to pursue a college education. I didn't know which way to go; I was eyeing to grab any opportunity that was going to come my way.

I enrolled myself in the American Institute of Banking and started taking courses at night. I was working hard, trying to take these courses to go to college. Due to my current situation, I knew getting a scholarship was impossible. I just kept taking courses at night, and it didn't matter how many years it would take to get a college degree because I intended to do that anyway. I knew I was born to be an accountant and was glad to find my passion finally.

While taking AIB courses, I met a lady who was an administrative assistant in the tax department. She saw me working hard every day and night and offered to help me out. Her husband was in the development department of Virginia Wesleyan College. He interviewed me, and I ended up getting a full scholarship for three years.

Since I had already been taking the AIB courses, I started out as a sophomore. I made straight A's in college, and even though Virginia Wesleyan did not have an accounting degree to offer, I enrolled in a liberal arts management degree.

After graduating from Virginia Wesleyan College with magna cum laude honors, I took a short break for about a year. I then took night courses for approximately five years at Old Dominion University. I finally got all the accounting courses I needed to sit for the CPA Exam.

My next stage was to clear the CPA exam; I knew it would be difficult. I took the Becker CPA Review Course (one of the best). I did everything they said to do, all the homework, all the reviews, even down to eating an apple the day of. I put my family on hold. Maybe to my detriment personally, but I did. I was going to do this one time. I could not subject myself to that misery again. I had to get on with my life.

Since I could not use a calculator or computer then, I had to rely on a pencil and paper to ace this exam. It was a four-day exam, and surprisingly, I passed all four parts on the first try. This was a major accomplishment, and I thank GOD Almighty for it.

I believe that if it weren't for that exam, I would not be the person I am today. By then, I had also developed a relationship with the Lord, which I believed was the high point of my life and helped me in my journey toward a better future.

Chapter Six — Love

"There is never a time or place for true love.
It happens accidentally, in a heartbeat, in a single flashing,
throbbing moment."

— **Sarah Dessen**

What is love? This is the question you ask yourself when nothing else makes sense, the answer to which may seemingly eliminate any doubt you have in your heart. Maybe love is an intense euphoria that gives you butterflies in your stomach. But at the same time, it may make your heart sink even at the slightest inconvenience. For some, it's just attachment, a mere sense of belonging, or just the idea of having someone with you through thick and thin. Or sometimes, it's just their presence that makes your heart go full. That's love — an amalgamation of millions of emotions in a single word.

The first person I thought I really loved was Jimmy, my first boyfriend. It would not be incorrect to say that our relationship was a roller-coaster ride filled with chaos, confusion, and lots of emotions. Only with time, I realized that it was not love — at least, not the kind of love I experienced later in my life.

We were both young and passionate, but now when I think back, I believe it was more of a physical relationship. I guess neither of us was crazily in love with one another, and the relationship ended when the two of us didn't need each other any longer. It was lust in the dust, literally.

It was only when I met my very first husband, Jerry, that I thought I had found love. It all happened unexpectedly; I had no idea I would end up marrying him. The first time I met Jerry was when he came to our house with my brother, who was in the Navy. Jerry was from Ohio, and he came to meet our family. Initially, I didn't even like him, but I guess he was attracted to me from the first time he saw me.

I was only sixteen then, still exploring myself and learning what my heart truly desired. By then, Jerry had visited our place at least three to four times. We used to have a lot of parties at our place where we would drink and smoke. At one such party, Jerry finally got a hold of me, and he kissed me. One thing led to another, and the next thing I knew was that we were in my bed, having sex. That was the night I lost my virginity; I vaguely remember seeing the blood stain on the sheets where we slept. It was the first time someone made me feel loved and alive. This was the beginning of our relationship, and I thought I was in love with him. However, it was only with time that I realized that what we had was not love because, initially, our relationship only involved having sex. Jerry had his own sports car, a TR6, but he never took me on a date, even after I fell in love with him and got pregnant with his child.

Although I didn't belong to a religious family, I had a shotgun wedding with Jerry after we learned that I was pregnant with his child. I remember the day we caught the bus because there was something wrong with Jerry's sports car. We arrived at the City Hall and got our license to make our relationship official just a day after my 18th birthday. At that time, I didn't even have my driver's license.

I wanted to tell my family that the two of us had gotten married even though we had not. But Jerry wanted us to get married even if the circumstances were not favorable. Eventually, we moved out and started living in our own apartment. The two of us would have a lot of friends over, and we partied a lot. Both of us were into drugs and drinking, and sex, and it continued throughout the three years of our marriage.

Life after marriage came with its own set of challenges and difficulties. The two of us had a little girl, and she turned out to be the most beautiful thing we had together. However, I believe our marriage was not meant to last, and it never did. I realized I did not want to get married to him. That is perhaps the reason things started going downhill.

Since Jerry got out of the military before we got married, he was never able to secure a good job after that, and it only added to our troubles. Our relationship became more problematic as we continued facing more challenges and struggled to tackle issues that came our way. We started having more fights than ever, and I remember one day, things got out of hand, and Jerry ended up hitting me. Something in me snapped! That was the moment when I knew something was not right, and I had to do something to make sure it didn't happen again.

Growing up in an abusive home where I saw my mother being abused for so many years, I knew it was not right for a man to hit his woman. I guess that was the turning point of our relationship; my love for Jerry in my heart began fading away, and I no longer felt attracted to him in the same passionate way.

I was very young and didn't know God back then. However, I believe that throughout this time, the Lord was watching over me, and I wasn't even aware of that. Once I put rat poison in the wine for Jerry but somehow ended up drinking it myself. I still do not know how but miraculously, I survived. That was the protection from my Lord — my savior, who was watching me while I was struggling to get my life straight.

It was the time when I was working at a bank. I loved my job and was determined to make a good future for myself. Unknowingly, I developed feelings for a guy named

Bernard, whom I had met a couple of times. I didn't know what got into me, but I remember I was totally smitten by his appearance and charm and his sex appeal.

At that time, I was out of school, had a daughter who was about three, and, yes, I was still married to Jerry. However, I realized that I was in love with Bernard and could not live without him.

Bernard was working at night in the computer room, and I would only get to see him in the morning when I went to work. The two of us used to get together during my lunch hour. As Bernard's sister lived close to where I worked, the two of us would often have sex at her house. We even met on the roof where I was working a couple of times to have sex and smoke weed. Eventually, Bernard got his own apartment, and we started spending more time together.

Once again, I believed I was in love. I guess that is what love meant to me at that time. For Bernard, I started avoiding my family and would not attend any events. It was my mom who eventually found out what was going on, and she told Jerry, which officially ended our marriage. It was me who left him even though there was nothing left in our marriage anyway.

Around this time, I purchased a Volkswagen, a really old one. I did not have a license, but I learned how to drive. I thought I had found love, and the next step was to get my life together. I was so focused on getting into college and taking AIB courses at night that I didn't even ask myself, what did Bernard want from me?

It's crazy how people manipulate you into believing that they love you only for their own personal gain. My heart shattered when I found out that Bernard only wanted me because he was trying to bring his daughter from New York. That's the reason why he wanted to be with me — to take care of his daughter. Our relationship didn't even last for one year, and I eventually returned home. I was having a mental breakdown at that time, but my mind was still able to function because I went to work every day. I stumbled upon a hard rock once again, but it didn't stop me from working toward my dreams.

I continued taking courses at night while taking care of my child all on my own. After having back-to-back setbacks in my love life, I realized sex was not love, and I had the two mixed up, which ultimately impacted the kind of choices I made. I dreaded being alone, and maybe that's why I accepted the love that came my way.

However, I do know now what love truly means. Love is when you cannot accomplish your dreams without that person because when you are in love, they become a true part of you. Mind, body, and soul — these things must be present to love someone, and that is what I tell young people who want to get married. I believe before making this big decision, there are some questions you may ask yourself; can you live without that person? Does this other person complete you? If that is not the way one feels about someone they want to marry, then it's just lust in the dust.

Eventually, I moved out to my own apartment — the place I loved with all my heart. I just knew that I was not meant to live by myself, not with the kind of sex drive I had. After I got to my apartment, I regretted sleeping with some of the guys I met with whom I should not have even been involved with in the first place.

I was in my early twenties when I met a nineteen-year-old guy. His name was Richie, and he had previously had relationships with other women. My sister, who was dating Richie's brother, hooked the two of us up. At that time, I had made up my mind that I was not going to sleep with just another guy. However, fate had other things planned for me, and ultimately, I realized that Richie was the love of my life.

I remember the first time when I met him; I didn't even want to talk to him or be around him. Since Richie didn't have a car, he walked me home that night and, later, took me out for dinner. In over ten years and after a failed marriage and a couple of relationships, I finally got to go on my first date, and it was beautiful. Richie made me question my own boundaries; at first, I had decided not to waste my time on men as I was about to quit my full-time job and start college. However, being with Richie made it all easy. We slept together for the first time two weeks after we met. He never went back home to Momma again.

There is no denying that Richie was head over heels in love with me. He was there when I went to college and graduated with honors. We were living together when I was featured in the newspaper. I did not mention him, but I could not have done it without him. I believe it was his love that made it possible for me to achieve everything. Richie loved me, and he loved my daughter; he treated her like she was his own. He took care of her in my absence and did all the things I could not do because I went to school, worked, and studied all the time. He was there to fill the gap, and I will always honor him, appreciate him and, yes, love him for what he did.

We lived together for five years, and I would say at the end of the fifth year, the Lord found me.

It was the beginning of a new journey for me. I gave my life to the Lord, and I knew that if it was not for Him, I could not have achieved what I did. Jesus Christ was the Lord of my life. I didn't want to upset my Lord anymore, so I told Richie that we could no longer live together like that.

Since Richie and I were in love, we decided to get married after five years. It was the beginning of something beautiful, and so many blessings came our way after that.

Richie had a decent job at that time; he had started out in a warehouse, where he first got promoted to counter sales, and later, he became the supervisor of counter sales in an electrical supply company.

My life revolved around Richie, my daughter, and my career. My family didn't want to have anything to do with me, and all eventually distanced themselves. They rejected me because I was different, but somewhere in my heart, I still loved them and cared about them. Although I had just started out on my spiritual journey, I felt grateful to be in the light while my family was adamant about staying in the dark. Regardless of all the differences, I wanted to be with them; however, I ultimately had to accept the harsh reality that they didn't want anything to do with me. Only my sister Twinkie stayed in touch with me, and I thanked the Lord for her presence in my life.

"And we know, that all things work together for the good, to them who love God, to them who are called according to his purpose

— Romans 8: 28 KJV

Richie and I had a beautiful marriage. However, the only problem was that he loved other women, and other women loved him. Problems hampered our relationship, but regardless of the problems, we tried to make it work. At that time, I was making more money than Richie as a CPA. Together, we bought our first house, and after we got married, we built a house in a very nice neighborhood. It was a four-bedroom house with a lawn. Richie loved cars, and he bought a Corvette and a Grand National, a Cadillac, and motorcycles and other vehicles. He loved to spend money, and I was very obliging. We both benefited from the blessings in our lives. I thought we were living a good life, but everything eventually turned ugly.

The incident that caused a strain in our relationship was when Richie interfered with a minor. Or the correct terminology is, contributing to the a delinquency of a minor. My daughter, Jewel, who was 12 then, revealed that he had touched her breasts. I didn't know how many times he did that before, but this time, he was taken to court. It was eventually ruled that either Richie or my daughter had to leave the house.

At this time, I was thankful to Richie's mother, Miss. Georgiana, for taking my daughter home and loving her. She took her to the necessary meetings and taught her everything. Richie was not incarcerated, however, he did go to a three months counseling session.

Years later, when my daughter and I had a conversation, she revealed that she had a problem with the fact that I stayed with Richie after she came out with the truth. However, all I can say is that I loved him and honored my vows. We eventually got over all of that, but it proved to be a strain on my relationship with Richie and with my daughter, and there was no chance it was going to be repaired easily.

Another time, I caught Richie talking to a woman on the telephone where he was telling her that he needed his *night nurse.* I remember I interrupted the conversation and threatened the woman and told her to stay away from my husband while I told Richie that I would be dealing with him later. The woman's husband died of an aneurysm two weeks later.

Around this time, I was working two and three jobs to help support our family. Richie had retired on disability by this time. Before retirement, he was working as a truck driver and would be home every single night. After his retirement, he would go off for the weekends and return on Monday or Tuesday.

However, ever since he retired, he would make excuses to be with other women, and I believe it continued for three years. I never doubted him when he said that he was going to North Carolina, where his male friend had a place. I just assumed that it was something to break the monotony. I didn't know that my husband was going to see another woman with whom he had an affair.

It hurt me a lot when I found out the truth. I loved him with all my heart and believed him when he claimed to love me too. I just couldn't stand the idea of him being with another woman. He was my husband, and together, we had taken vows to be there for each other. I thought this superseded everything and everybody. People used to talk about the kind of love Richie and I shared for decades. But even though we were together for thirty years, there was always a hint of infidelity through the years.

I will say this: through all the drug addictions, we overcame; through all the infidelities, we overcame; through all the money issues, we overcame — we lived, we loved, we went to Church together and ministered together. We vacationed in the Caribbean for many years. All I have to say is, regardless, life was good.

A songwriter once quoted, "As long as all of my good days out weight my bad days, I won't complain." I adapted, and God Almighty blessed us.

Richie was the love of my life at that time, and now, he is deceased — gone forever. After his death, some people thought that I had him cremated because I didn't want anybody to visit him. But that is not why I did it; I just didn't want to see him closed up in a box underground.

After his death, I sold the house and moved into a condo. Soon, I became involved in a relationship that I shouldn't have had in the first place. Again, was that love? I mean, I really thought that I loved that man. I wanted him, and I needed help. He helped me a great deal to navigate "life after Richie." His name was Marcus; however, since he was not available, our relationship came to an end after three years. At that time, I didn't want anyone else. But life had other plans.

"He who finds a wife finds a good thing
and obtains favor from the LORD."

— Proverbs 18:22, ESV

When my current husband found me and showed me what it is like to love in the way of the Lord, my belief in love was reinvigorated. He loves me as much as I love the Lord. Moreover, he loves the Lord for himself, not to please me. He is the genuine one, and I love him; it's like we both are meant to be together. Our married life has been beautiful so far. All of my life, I wanted to have a husband to worship and praise the Lord beside me in church. I feel grateful now that it is finally happening. Rick, my husband, is a GOD send, and I really thank the Lord for sending him into my life. Rick courted me and dated me. We had a lovely wedding at a very large church. I finally got the chance to wear a white wedding gown. Rick managed to sweep me off my feet with little love, and I love him for that. It was the beginning of our beautiful journey together.

Since we married four months after meeting each other online, there have been good days, and we've had a few bad days, but fortunately for us, the good outweighs the bad. Our bond of love has grown and continues to grow ever stronger each day.

Chapter Seven — Where's the menu?

Motherhood

"I will look after you, and I will look after anybody you say needs to be looked after, any way you say. I am here. I brought my whole self to you. I am your mother."

— Maya Angelou

My daughter, my only child, truly believed that I was the worst mother there could ever be. Sadly, as heartbreaking as it sounds, I had no reason or justification to prove her otherwise.

Now that I think back through the decades, I realize I really was a bad mother. I got pregnant when I had no plans for the future, and the idea of *living my life to the fullest* was all messed up in my head. Motherhood was not planned for me; it was a result of having unprotected sex, which was not something unusual for me.

Regardless of the fact that I was quite young with no plans for the future or a penny to my name, I was happy to continue the pregnancy and have this child. The word *abortion* was not even in my vocabulary at that time. For the young, energetic me, pregnancy was yet another adventure, and I looked forward to carrying a child that I hoped would turn out to be a reflection of me. That idea was pretty much the reason why I was so determined to have the baby while I was still struggling to set the course of my life straight.

My journey toward embracing motherhood was another story. It would not be incorrect to say that it was a rough ride. However, I truly believe in the utmost significance of the role that a mother plays in the life of her child. A mother goes through so many changes, physically and mentally, to become a new person and find immense strength, tolerance, and patience to give birth to a new life that they hope will grow up to become just like them. There is no love among humans that can ever match or exceed the unconditional love of a mother. They have the power to nurture a life inside them before they bring them into the world.

From pregnancy to childbirth, the journey of motherhood is beautiful if only one is able to make the most out of it.

Sadly, I hardly recall any memories of the day I got pregnant. As I mentioned earlier, I was not on any contraceptives, and my pregnancy was a result of unprotected sex. I hated having sex with condoms! However, I do remember the day when I told the father-to-be that I was pregnant with his child. It was a beautiful day, but given how the circumstances changed between us over the years, it is heartbreaking to think back to it now.

On the other hand, when my family found out that I was pregnant, I was told to get married right away. My dad thought if he was good enough to lay with, he was good enough to marry. Especially since Jerry wanted to marry me. *That's what you gotta do! You gotta get married.* Those were his words, and at that time, I didn't really have anything to say. I knew I had no other choice and had to do it one way or the other.

During the first few months of my pregnancy, I was still in school. Later on, when I got married in September and started living with my husband, I started working. It was tough to manage it all together, but I don't know how

I managed to pull everything off. Once again, I did what I had to do.

That was the time when it was all kind of fuzzy. As much as I would like to think that it was all full of joy and happiness, the memories contradict the fantasy. Those were tough times. I didn't have maternity clothes to wear, and with time, I could no longer fit into the clothes I already had. Moreover, I didn't have much of an income at that time to buy new clothes either. I remember there was one dashiki that I used to wear a lot. The design of the material was headshots of many of the black activists of the time. Malcolm X, Martin Luther King, Jesse Jackson, Angela Davis, Megar Edwards, Rosa Parks, etc. My brother brought it, and I absolutely loved it. I know I kept it for at least twenty years just because it bought back so many memories.

Life was a roller coaster; some days were easier, but the others were incredibly hard. I did remember that my pregnancy was a wild thing. I was rebellious, but, in some ways, I did want to be a flower child. I would have been at Woodstock, but I did not travel anywhere. I was a wild child. I smoked pot and drank during my whole pregnancy. However, circumstances did not allow me to become a flower child.one. I continued living my life the same way I had before — seeking pleasure in things that were not good for me. Even when I was pregnant, it didn't stop me from smoking cigarettes, pot and doing drugs. I guess at that time, I just did what I felt like doing. If it felt good, then do it! Wrong, Wrong, Wrong!

I eventually graduated from high school and landed my first real job. I worked at a savings and loan Company. It was a totally white environment, but I was treated fairly as far as I was concerned. I was just so thankful to have a decent job. I caught the bus to and from work every day. I was so focused on building a life for myself that I didn't even realize that the day was finally here when I was ready to bring forth a new life into this world. It was one usual day when I went to the store and didn't even realize I was having contractions. But soon, it became clear, and I was rushed to the hospital. On December 25th, I gave birth to Jewel, my only daughter, after staying in labor for about seven hours. She was a premature baby and weighed only four pounds and six ounces, and I didn't get any stitches because she was a very small child.

Her dad visited me in the hospital, and I let him name her *Jewel LaShaun.* I was not sure where he came up with the name, but I thought it was beautiful.

Surprisingly, I never had to pay for the hospital, and they didn't bill anything under my name either. I never had to pay the doctor's fee for the few prenatal visits that I had during my pregnancy, either. Jewel was kept in the hospital for about two weeks to a month before the doctors allowed us to take her home. However, we weren't even charged for that. I like to think that it was a gift from God because she was born on Christmas Day, even though I had not found my true path then.

Motherhood came with a lot of responsibilities, some of which were beyond my comprehension. I believe I still had a long way to go before I could learn what it truly meant to have a child of your own.

Growing up, Jewel was a very bright child, very intelligent. However, she did have some sort of affinity for fires, or as I like to say, she was a firebug. One time, she burned the Christmas tree, and the other time, she set the wood next to the fireplace on fire. I was worried about her initially, and I believed she did all those things to get our attention. She eventually stopped doing that as she got older, and I thank the Lord for that.

I believe Jewel missed out on a lot of things when her father and I separated at the age of four. He never paid any child support and only visited Jewel a couple of times before he disappeared.

During this time, I came to understand real hunger, real destitution, and not knowing where to turn. I remember if it had not been for a neighbor seeing my destitute state and giving me some food to eat, I think I would have starved. At this time, I lived so far from my family, with no transportation or money. All I remember was walking to my father's house, pushing a stroller in the summertime. I must have walked five miles. "I did what I had to do". This was my motto. Once again, the Lord stepped in and provided.

Although I moved on with my life, Jewel's father never married again or had any other kids. His life was so messed up as he had become addicted to drugs and alcohol. I was still the love of his life when he died forty years later.

Being a single mother was difficult, but it didn't stop me from having the most fun in my life. I enrolled in school, started a job, and had a few love affairs. I thought I was living the best life, but now that I think about it, it was just an illusion of my mind – there was nothing great about it.

Jewel was my only child, and I should have done everything in my power to protect her. She was a bright child — the sunshine of my life. However, I was not there to shield her when she was abused at the age of 12 by my then-husband, Richie. Even after she told me how he tried to take advantage of her, I did nothing to confront her abuser. Instead, I ended up sending Jewel to live with Ms. Georgiana, Richie's mother.

We have already discussed in the previous chapter how I chose to stay with my husband despite knowing that he abused my daughter because I was in *love*. The court had ordered that both could not be in the same house, and I chose my husband before my daughter.

This led to Jewel acting out. Among other things that she had to get through, she thought I had abandoned her, and she didn't like it. I believe this incident shattered our relationship to irreparable measure.

When Jewel turned 18, she eventually came back to live with me while I was still married to Richie. As the saying goes, *the fruit does not fall far from the tree*; Jewel grew up into a wild child. Going through a similar phase, I tried my best to be compassionate with her but to tell you the truth, I did not do everything in my power to repair the broken relationship I had with my daughter. I had failed to protect her when she needed me the most, which eventually caused more problems in our relationship.

Being a wild child, Jewel would often disappear for days as she, too, liked to live her life on the edge. By then, we had started living a pretty decent life, but somehow, Jewel would find a way to spend time with those who were still living below the poverty line.

When she finally graduated from high school, I was relieved. I was willing to pay for her college as I wanted her to make a life for herself. I wanted her to go to a local college, as we had many near our place, but none worked out. Although Jewel was smart, that was not what she wanted to do.

During this time, I was fully focused on building a career. Most of the time, I would stay busy at work, and I had also actively started spending more time at the church, which I believed helped out tremendously. I guess because of all of these activities, I could never give Jewel enough time or attention, which widened the gap that existed between us.

Jewel was smart, and she had various jobs. However, just like her mother, she loved men and was in relationship after relationship. She had two kids, Simone and Davon, with a man who was a drug dealer and addict and was in and out of jail. Later, when Jewel found out that the guy was having babies with other women, she decided to leave him and the kids.

I believe it must have been a tough decision for her, but she did what she had to do at that time. It was Ms. Georgiana who suggested that I take custody of the children, who were about four and six at that time. Although I didn't want to raise any more children, I saw it as a second chance to redeem myself after everything I was not able to do for Jewel.

I had no trouble getting custody of Simone and Davon. The two brightened our lives, and my husband Richie absolutely loved them. He spoiled them and would give them anything they asked for. Meanwhile, his mother, Ms. Georgiana, once again helped me raise them as I was working a full-time and two part-time jobs.

It was a new experience for me, and I tried to do everything for Simone and Davon that I couldn't do for Jewel. I raised them until they were in high school, and they became a very important part of my life.

That's when I was hit by something unexpected. When the kids were in their teenage years and wanted to live their own way, Jewel decided to take back custody. It was I who raised them and taught them how to live a good life. However, whatever Jewel decided to do later on ended up dismantling all my efforts.

I believe it was a test for me. I realized long ago that my relationship with Jewel could have been better. I took care of her kids and didn't ask for anything in return. All I wanted was forgiveness for everything I did to her. Moreover, I asked Davon and Simone to forgive me for anything I may have done to them. I tried to do my best in the situation that I was given.

Although Richie is now dead, I wish he had been here to see the mess that Davon and Simone made out of their lives.

I look at Simone, and she looks just like me. She is now 25 and has two kids. She is a beautiful girl, and even though I do not agree with the decisions she made in her life, I know in my heart that she will straighten out her life one day.

On the other hand, Davon is living in the state of Washington and is about to enter his thirties. Although he is not living an ideal life, I just thank the Lord that he is not in jail, knowing what he has been doing with his life.

My daughter Jewel is now working in the security department at a hospital close to where she lives. I'm glad that she has realized that her happiness does not lie in young men.

While I thank the Lord for allowing me to see the right path and helping me straighten out my life, my heart never stops praying for my grandchildren.

My heart breaks to see the two children I raised in such situations. I believe there is so much better for them out here than where they are right now. I know that there are a lot of temptations and the children have got themselves involved in all sorts of activities. I hope that one day, Simone and Davon find the path that will guarantee eternal peace and happiness in their lives.

Chapter Eight — Career

"Your success in your career will be in direct proportion to what you do after you've done what you are expected to do."

— **Brian Tracy**

When I reflect back on my teenage years, there's one particular experience that stands out in my mind. That was the incident that shaped my journey toward independence and responsibility. It changed my perspective on my life.

At the tender age of 16, while still attending high school, I embarked on an exciting learning adventure. It was my very first job at Lerner Shops. I still remember the excitement and nervousness that coursed through my veins as I donned a red banner, proudly displaying the words "Miss Charge it," just like the iconic Miss America herself.

Armed with a clipboard and a stack of applications, I was entrusted with the important task of approaching customers and inquiring about their possession of a Lerner Shop credit card. For those who didn't have one, it was my duty to gracefully assist them in filling out the necessary paperwork to acquire this coveted piece of financial freedom.

As time went on, my role within the company evolved. I found myself working in the credit department, gaining insight into the intricate workings of financial transactions. During my time as a cashier at Lerner Shops, the true nature of my job unfolded, revealing a plethora of fascinating moments and unexpected discoveries.

There were days when weariness would weigh heavy on my young shoulders. Yet, even in those moments, I found solace in the vast expanse of the store, discovering secret nooks and crannies where I could steal a moment of respite. Hidden away, I could recharge, gather my thoughts, and prepare for the next wave of customers eager to embark on their own shopping adventures.

Upon graduating from high school, my path naturally led me toward a new chapter of my life. Equipped with the valuable skills of shorthand and typing that I had acquired in school, I set my sights on the real world. This was one thing I contributed to my father's leading. He had a shorthand book at home; I don't know where he got it from, but he insisted I should take up this skill. Thanks, Dad; this is one good thing you did right.

My first official job after high school was with a savings and loans institution, although these institutions soon became a part of history. In this new realm, I joined the ranks of the accounting department as a junior secretary, where the familiar rhythms of typing and shorthand often consumed my days.

Of course, that job didn't last too long for me. I started working in June, and by December, I made the difficult decision to quit. The reason behind my departure was an incredibly joyous one — I had welcomed my first and only child into the world. Becoming a parent changed everything for me, and I knew that my priorities had shifted.

Nevertheless, that job was quite intriguing to me because it allowed me to work in an office setting — an environment I had always aspired to be a part of. Specifically, I was assigned to the accounting department and found myself drawn to the world of numbers. Whenever I wasn't typing away, I would often be engrossed in inputting various data and figures. During this time, I realized my affinity for working with numbers.

After the birth of my child, my life took a different path. I no longer had to commute on the bus to reach my workplace, as my responsibilities as a mother took precedence. Looking back, I remember vividly being the only black person in that office, which created a sense of uniqueness and, at times, unease. It wasn't an ideal situation, but it seemed to mirror the experiences I had encountered throughout my life. It was as though those experiences had been preparing me for the challenges I would face in the future.

Following my decision to leave that job and with the arrival of my child, I transitioned back to more modest roles, such as working in Lerner Shops and handling cashier duties. It was during this time that I began to reassess my career aspirations. However, a significant breakthrough occurred roughly a year later when I embarked on a new journey — working for a bank.

This bank has undergone several name changes over the years, from Virginia National Bank to Sovereign Bank to Nations Bank, and finally settling on its current name, Bank of America. Within the bank's installment loan department, I found myself once again surrounded by numbers. During this period, I began to realize my innate talent and knack for working with figures.

Back then, I remember how things were. Job opportunities were posted, and you could apply for them. During that time, I stumbled upon a job opening that caught my interest. It led me to the Bank Reconciliation Department, a place filled with fascinating tasks and challenges. I spent some time there, but little did I know that my destiny lay elsewhere, specifically in the trust tax department. It was there that I gained invaluable experience in handling trust tax returns.

I wasn't hired as a technical expert in trust tax matters when I first joined the trust tax department. E. Randolf

Fraser, Jr., I will always love and respect you for believing in me and giving me a chance. And you kept re- hiring me back over the years until I did not need you anymore. Thank you. Instead, my skills in typing and shorthand landed me a position where I processed returns and performed various other duties. There was a lady who was Randy's administrative assistant, Pauline Patterson. She saw something in me — perhaps, my underlying potential that I could not see myself at that time. She recognized that I was a single mother juggling night school alongside my work. Her belief in me was unwavering.

As fate would have it, her husband was involved in the development of a college that needed to diversify its student body. Consequently, they were offering scholarships specifically to black individuals. I was fortunate enough to be chosen as a recipient and was granted a full scholarship. It was a remarkable opportunity that enabled me to pursue my dreams without the burden of financial constraints. Thank God for Affirmative Action.

After completing my education, armed with my Liberal Arts Management degree, I returned to the trust tax department, albeit temporarily. I continued preparing tax returns and handling various responsibilities related to my field. During that time, I couldn't help but recall the lofty dreams I once held. I envisioned myself achieving great things and significantly impacting my chosen profession. Yet, deep down, I knew that obtaining an accounting degree was crucial to realizing those aspirations.

I never imagined that my career path would lead me to Accounting. Back when I was in college, the institution I attended didn't offer any specialized accounting degree. However, I was determined to pursue my passion, so I enrolled in all the accounting courses available to me.

After completing college, I realized I needed more accounting knowledge and expertise. I understood that to excel in this field, I had to go above and beyond. So, I took it upon myself to pursue additional courses outside of college. I was determined to succeed, and nothing was going to stand in my way.

It was during this time that I stumbled upon a job opportunity in the trust tax department. It seemed like fate had intervened because that position felt like the missing piece of the puzzle. It was the moment when I discovered my true calling.

Deep down in my heart, I knew I was meant to work in accounting. The idea of being an accountant became my ultimate goal, even if it meant facing countless challenges and hurdles along the way.

I didn't have all the answers or know the full extent of what lay ahead, but I had an unwavering resolve. I possessed a can-do attitude that propelled me forward, no matter what obstacles stood in my path. I was committed to doing whatever it took to achieve my dreams. There was a fire within me, a burning desire to make my mark in the accounting world.

Looking back, I realize that my journey into accounting was not a mere coincidence. It felt like a divine hand was guiding me every step of the way.

After completing my education, I found myself working for a man named Fred Martin, who worked from home. He became my mentor and taught me the intricacies of bookkeeping and insurance, areas that weren't covered in my college curriculum. I will forever be grateful to Fred for his guidance and the invaluable lessons he imparted to me. Although the compensation wasn't substantial, I poured my heart and soul into my work, knowing it would help me get closer to my goals.

From there, I sought out opportunities to gain more experience. I remember my time at a savings and loan institution, where I worked in the finance department. It was there that I delved into the world of tracking mortgage-backed bonds and learned about investments and accounting practices related to them. At the time, I had no idea how this knowledge would prove invaluable in shaping my future career. Looking back, I believe that every step I took, every experience I gained, and every person I met significantly shaped my path. It was a series of fortunate events and a relentless pursuit of knowledge that led me to where I am today.

Then there was this amazing little company, and it just so happened that one of the women involved in it is still a dear friend of mine today. When she started working part-time for this pharmaceutical company, she discovered their books were in an absolute mess. They had no idea just how rapidly they had grown. It all began as a humble mom-and-pop business, a true family affair. But their success had taken them by surprise, and they found themselves struggling to keep up.

Thankfully, fate intervened, and I had the opportunity to step in and lend a hand alongside my friend. Despite having a full-time job during the day, I was determined to help them sort out their financial chaos. So, night after night, I dedicated myself to their cause.

It was an enormous challenge, the biggest mess I had ever encountered. Their growth had been so rapid that their operations had become unwieldy. But with perseverance and relentless effort, we managed to bring order to their financial records. I ensured they knew the full extent of their receivables, payables, and everything else. Moreover, I played a crucial role in implementing a robust accounting system to serve them well into the future. In those moments, I became more than just an accountant. I was the office manager, the go-to person for all things financial.

Not only did I bring order to their books, but I also took charge of hiring and firing, fully embracing my newfound responsibilities. Suddenly, it felt like the perfect position for me — a role where I could make a real impact. Through this experience, I learned a valuable lesson: hard work truly pays off, regardless of the circumstances surrounding you. Even though it was a family-owned business and there were challenges lurking in the background, I remained steadfast in doing my job to the best of my abilities.

Their appreciation for my dedication and commitment was unwavering. They recognized my potential and generously offered to sponsor my CPA review course. I eagerly accepted their support. Fueled by their belief in me, I embarked on the journey to become a certified public accountant.

As destiny would have it, I triumphed over the CPA exam, a testament to the perseverance instilled in me during those transformative years with the pharmaceutical company.

Once I achieved my goal, I knew it was time to move on, but the bond between us remained strong. They had been good to me, and in return, I had poured my heart and soul into their company, leaving behind a legacy of excellence. That experience became a turning point in my life, a moment where I realized that I could accomplish anything my heart desired with determination.

There were indeed numerous challenges I faced on my journey to success. Looking back, I can confidently say that it wasn't an easy road. I was determined to make something of myself, so I took on two or even three jobs at a time, tirelessly working day and night. It was a period of constant learning, where I absorbed knowledge and skills without knowing exactly where they would lead me.

I vividly remember when I started my little tax practice. Armed with just a calculator, pencil, ink pen, and tax forms, I would visit people's homes to prepare their tax returns right there with them. I was willing to do whatever it took to succeed. Each day was a step forward as I worked diligently, honing my abilities and striving to become better at what I did.

During that time, I also had the privilege of working for the church. I embraced my faith in my early twenties and joined their ranks. It was a beautiful period where good things happened, and personal growth flourished. Although my job options seemed limited at that point, my aspirations soared high. One dream, in particular, was to work for CBN, and against all odds, I managed to secure a position in their accounting department. I went from being an accountant to a senior accountant for Operation Blessing, which brought me great satisfaction.

However, amidst these triumphs, I faced a significant hurdle that was deeply disheartening: racism. It pains me to acknowledge that at CBN, there were noticeable disparities in how black people were treated. I still recall one particular incident that remains etched in my memory. I applied for a position that I had always dreamed of — the assistant controller role. The controller who had initially hired me recognized my potential and planned for me to eventually take on that position, as I had all the required experience.

But let me tell you, my journey to this point was anything but easy. I started my career as an accountant, a senior accountant, to be exact. It wasn't a typical entry-level position. In fact, my boss had to get special permission to bring me on board because he had already hired another accountant. When I found out that I was the second accountant he brought in, I was determined to prove my worth.

I came from a diverse background, with experience in insurance, investments, and taxation. I was well-equipped to handle the responsibilities of any accounting director, yet despite my skills and expertise, I found myself stuck in the same position year after year. I remained at the company, the Christian Broadcasting Company, from 1997 until around 2005. The frustration of being overlooked for promotions grew, but I didn't let it dampen my spirit.

Then, out of the blue, everything changed. One day, I was casually browsing online when I stumbled upon an incredible opportunity. There it was — a job posting for the controller position at a company that was setting up operations in our area. Without hesitation, I submitted my application, not knowing what the future held for me. Little did I know, things were about to move at lightning speed.

A short while later, I received a call from a woman who sounded excited and energetic. "This is gonna move pretty fast. Are you ready?" she told me.

I braced myself for what she had to say next. "We're going to start with a telephone interview tomorrow, and if they like you, you'll be invited for a face-to-face interview." The pace was exhilarating, and I eagerly embraced the challenge.

As fate would have it, the interviews went exceptionally well, and before I knew it, I found myself in a new job — one where I was not just tolerated but truly appreciated. Tracey Velde (TV), thank you for taking a chance on me. Thank you for giving me a chance to excel. I was appointed as the assistant manager of the department, and it was a breath of fresh air. Finally, I had the opportunity to supervise an accounting staff, and I reveled in the responsibility.

Although I wasn't the controller of that particular branch due to my lack of experience in the Department of Defense (DOD), it didn't matter to me at that time. I loved every aspect of my new role, and surprisingly, my enthusiasm was reciprocated. The synergy between my team and me was undeniable. It was as if all the hardships, the setbacks, and the lessons I had learned throughout my career had led me to this moment.

Time passed, and as luck would have it, my boss decided to retire. This was my chance to step up and take on a greater role. I seized the opportunity with unwavering determination and dedication. The company specialized in property management, and I found myself truly passionate about my job. It was the cream of the crop, offering a handsome salary and a sense of autonomy.

I believe the reason why TV hired me goes back to a moment in the interview that still resonates with me today. As we sat across from each other, she sifted through a stack of applications and asked me a thought-provoking question, "With so many qualified candidates, what will make me remember you?"

In response, I confidently replied, "I will make you look good." That marked the beginning of my tenure at Lincoln Military Housing, a job I truly cherished. I have to give a shout-out to Francesca Connor, aka Franny Pants. She was the hardest-working woman at Lincoln. She was a hard taskmaster, but she was my friend. Thank you for the many evenings and nights we labored together. Simply because the job had to get done.

While I hesitate to say that I retired from there, it was more of a conscious decision to step away from the workforce. I yearned for a change — a chance to pursue my own endeavors from the comfort of my home. Reflecting on my journey, I feel immense pride in my accomplishments thus far.

One of my most significant achievements was graduating college with honors. It was a culmination of years of dedication, late-night study sessions, and a burning desire to excel. Additionally, I conquered the formidable CPA exam on my first attempt. The feeling of triumph upon passing was nothing short of exhilarating. It was a testament to my perseverance and unwavering commitment to personal growth.

Throughout my various roles, I always sought opportunities to uplift my community. I understood the struggles my fellow individuals faced, and it compelled me to lend a helping hand wherever possible. I recognized that not everyone had access to the financial expertise they desperately needed, so I took it upon myself to assist them with investments, tax returns, and overall financial management. I had been extraordinarily fortunate, and I felt compelled to pay it forward.

From a humble position of merely asking people to complete job applications, I gradually climbed the professional ladder to become the accounting manager for a thriving business. Managing an entire accounting department was a momentous achievement in my career. It affirmed that my relentless drive and genuine desire to make a difference had propelled me forward.

Chapter Nine — Suicide

*"Some losses in life hunt you and hurt
you forever until you are dead."*

— Unknown

Jeffrey, or as we fondly called him, Bop, held a special place in my heart as the last boy sandwiched between the three little children in our family. Bop and I shared a unique bond, one that transcended blood ties. He wasn't physically or mentally handicapped, but his true challenge lay in the environment he had to endure day in and day out.

In school, Bop achieved decent grades, but it seemed like no one really noticed him. Seeing him overlooked, his potential buried beneath indifference, broke my heart. Bop was born in 1967, and for the first seven years of his life, I was there by his side, trying my best to take care of him. Growing up, I was still finding my own way, but looking after him was something I embraced wholeheartedly. Despite the difficulties, he was a beautiful child, and caring for him never felt like a burden. He was my baby brother.

However, as time past, life became unbearable for Bop. The world around him turned dark, and he found himself trapped in the clutches of adversity. Yet, through it all, my love for him remained unwavering. I loved him with every fiber of my being because Bop possessed a unique light that radiated from within. This essence drew people towards him, inspiring an outpouring of affection from those lucky enough to know him.

I still vividly recall an incident that weighs heavy on my conscience. Bop was just a year old when I accidentally dropped him in our basement, the cold cement floor serving as an unforgiving landing spot. At that terrifying moment, he lost consciousness, and we rushed him to the hospital in a frenzy. I thank the heavens that he emerged from that ordeal unscathed, with no lasting mental effects. It was a frightening reminder of the fragile nature of life, and I silently vowed to protect him from harm, no matter the cost.

Years later, I had many heartfelt conversations with my brothers, trying to put into words the kind of upbringing we had. It was interesting how they described it as if we were part of the Addams family, you know, that quirky, spooky bunch. But for me, it was much simpler. It was just a bad environment, plain and simple.

Imagine growing up in a place where nobody cared about you or took a genuine interest in who you were or what you needed. It was like being swept along by a powerful current, lost and forgotten. Maybe it had something to do with the alcoholism and drugs that plagued our home. One of my brothers even called it *demons* lurking in our midst. I don't know about that, but I do know that it wasn't a nurturing environment for any child to grow up in.

When you are surrounded by such negativity and chaos, it starts to seep into your very being. It wears you down, bit by bit. Gone were the carefree days of playing outside with my brothers, laughing, and having a blast. Growing up in that environment forced me to mature faster than I should have. I couldn't help but think deeply about life and our circumstances.

Then there was our father, who was a mess back then. Most of the time, he would be found stumbling around the house, completely intoxicated. I remember how my mother would reel with frustration and anger, and her children would be caught in the middle of their constant battles. It was far from a conducive atmosphere for anyone's well-being.

School life was no escape either. Nobody cared about Bop there, either. It was no wonder that eventually, around ninth or tenth grade, he just couldn't take it anymore. The weight of it all became too much, and he dropped out, as expected. It was tough to recount those memories and emotions, but it was essential to acknowledge where we come from. Bop wasn't just any child; he was my brother, and deep down, I knew he had goodness in him. I can't say for certain that he was doing drugs, but I did notice him drinking a bit. Still, that didn't define him. What defined him were the challenges he faced, and it breaks my heart to admit that he was born into the wrong family at the wrong time.

One of my other brothers once confessed, "I left them."

Those words have haunted me ever since. I managed to escape that chaotic environment as soon as I could, leaving them all behind. I had a shotgun wedding and built a life of my own, rarely looking back. I did visit them afterward, but it was never the same as being there.

I was so caught up in my own world — my family, my husband, my child, my career — that I failed to see the pain and desperation my brothers and sisters lived with. I left them behind, focused on building my own life and pursuing my own dreams, and turned a blind eye to the hurt that consumed them. I regret not being there for Bop, not offering him the love, care, and attention he desperately needed.

He faced his demons alone, with no support system to lean on. I had cared for my younger siblings when I was at home, but he had no one to care for him. He was left to bear his burdens in solitude in my absence. Nobody else seemed to care about him; he was overlooked and forgotten.

It feels like just yesterday, but my last conversation with him took place way back in 1988. At that time, I was fully immersed in my work within the Church, tirelessly spreading the message of light and hope to those who would listen. I always believed that the Lord's blessings were showered upon me more abundantly for them to see.

One particular memory from that time still stings deep within my heart. My brother, with a tinge of bitterness, once remarked, "Your dogs live better than we do."

Those words pierced through me, but they also sparked something inside me. I began to realize that if I could find a way out of that pit, then surely my family could too. They just needed to open their hearts to the Gospel of Christ and witness its transformative power in their life.

However, I soon came to understand that it was not within my control to make them accept the Lord. Each individual had to make that choice for themselves. Unfortunately, they showed little interest in embracing the path I had found. It was painful for me to watch as their lives spiraled further away from the light. It seemed as though Satan himself had wreaked havoc on their existence.

Of course, there were some of us who managed to break free from the chains of our past and step into a brighter future. But even for us, the scars of our former lives remained etched upon our souls. The weight of our family's history seemed to drag us down, a constant reminder of the pain we had endured. It still hurts me to this very day to reflect upon those dark times when our parents battled alcoholism.

I often wonder what troubled Bop. Perhaps it was the influence of our other siblings who struggled with drug addiction and alcoholism. Somehow, their choices impacted him, and in that final conversation we shared, he confessed, "I don't wanna grow up to be like my brothers."

I believe he felt trapped, having no other options, no other paths to choose.

He poured his energy into building his physical strength, hoping that a chiseled physique would somehow compensate for the turmoil within. But when he passed away, seeing him lying there lifeless in his coffin tore me apart inside.

I longed for Bop to embrace Christ with all his heart. I yearned for him to find solace and salvation in the arms of our Savior. I often wondered if there was a chance for him to come and stay with me, to escape the darkness that surrounded him. But deep down, I knew he didn't desire that. He was on his own journey, making his own choices, even if they led him astray.

I'll never forget the pain that washed over me when I heard his heartbreaking words. He uttered those five dreaded words that nobody ever wants to hear: "I don't want to live." It hit me hard, like a punch to the gut. He had tried to take his own life multiple times before, using carbon monoxide as his weapon. But tragically, the third attempt succeeded. It happened on his 21st birthday, a day that should have been filled with celebration and hope. Instead, it became a chilling reminder of the darkness that consumed him.

It should have brought our family together like a rallying cry to support and protection. But instead, it drove us apart. We were once so close as children, but now the distance between us seemed insurmountable. It was as if our bonds had been shattered, scattered into irreparable fragments. I felt lost, thrown for a loop by the enormity of it all.

When the time came, I knew I had a responsibility. I had to gather the strength to organize his funeral, a somber event that would serve as our final farewell. And yet, even in death, my mom couldn't bring herself to attend. It wasn't held in a traditional funeral home but in my church. My heart ached as I watched her absence speak volumes. At that moment, it felt like her love for me had evaporated, replaced by an unexplained resentment.

Perhaps she was simply blinded by her own struggles. She battled with her health, fighting against diabetes, enduring the painful amputation of half her foot, and wrestling with high blood pressure. But deep down, I knew these physical ailments were just manifestations of the hatred festering within her. Despite it all, I loved my mom fiercely. Even now, long after her passing in '97, that love continues to grow with each passing year.

I refuse to place blame on either of my parents. It wasn't their fault; the circumstances that engulfed us all. Life dealt us a difficult hand, and we did our best to navigate the storm. Their flaws and shortcomings were overshadowed by their immense love for their troubled child. They, too, felt the weight of the situation, and in their own imperfect ways, they tried to protect him. And for that, I cannot fault them.

How did we ever find our way back from the depths of such darkness? Truth be told, we haven't fully recovered. The wounds inflicted upon us by our own father still linger, etched deeply in our souls. I vividly remember the day my little sister, so innocent and vulnerable, had to summon every ounce of strength to fend off his advances. Those horrific encounters left her scarred with a lasting torment that haunts her to this very day.

As for my oldest brother, he managed to escape the clutches of our father's malevolence. He was fortunate enough to evade the nightmare that engulfed our family. On the other hand, my oldest sister never found solace from the abuse she endured. It clung to her like a relentless shadow, gnawing at her spirit until it ultimately claimed her life. The weight of her suffering was simply too much to bear.

Then there was Paul, somewhat of an outcast within the family. He stood apart, carrying the burdens of our shared past. Though he led a solitary existence, there was a quiet strength within him.

As for me, I struggled to define my place in this tumultuous journey. I often found solace in solitude, but I am far from being a mere loner. Deep down, I am filled with love for myself and for others, capable of bringing joy and light to those around me. Many see me as the life of the party, a beacon of happiness.

But the truth is the scars of my past run deep, forever marked by the presence of my late brother, Roger. His absence, his tragic demise, weighs heavily upon me. They say he took his own life in that city jail, but my brother Paul insists that there's more to the story, that something darker was at play. And then there was Donald, the one who drowned his sorrows in alcohol, a path that led him to a tragic end. The Army couldn't save him, and in the end, he succumbed to his demons.

Bernard, another casualty of our tormented history, lost his friends and found himself confined to the sterile walls of a nursing home where he died alone. ClarenceFats, or CW somehow, he managed to piece his life back together, yet he remains a solitary figure, never fully free from the chains of our shared past. As for Bop, he is no longer with us; his pain and suffering were finally laid to rest. Twinkie, well, she seems to have found her way, at least on the surface. But deep down, we all bear the scars that refuse to heal.

So, no, we haven't truly recovered. But in our collective journey, we continue to fight, to search for moments of peace and healing. We hold onto the flickering hope that one day, we may find the serenity we so desperately seek.

Our lives were shattered, and the pieces were scattered far and wide. It was a constant struggle, a relentless battle to reclaim our peace and rebuild what was broken. We had to find a way to carry on without letting our painful past consume us.

The path to healing lay in surrendering myself to a higher power. I gave my life to the Lord, seeking solace and guidance in my darkest moments. It was the only way I could bear the weight of what I had endured. And though it wasn't an instant fix, faith became the foundation that anchored my soul.

Then there was Twinkie, a beacon of unwavering strength and resilience. She poured her heart and soul into raising her three boys, sparing no effort to ensure they received a college education. It was her way of shielding them from the chains of her past and giving them a fighting chance to shape their destiny. We were determined not to let our history dictate our future.

Yet, despite our best efforts, we remain haunted. The ghosts of our past continue to linger, whispering their haunting echoes in our ears. It was a constant reminder that the wounds may have scabbed over, but the scars ran deep. We are marked by our experiences, forever carrying the weight of what we've been through.

Chapter Ten — Legacy

"Leaving behind a legacy is not about engraving your name in stone, but about etching your essence into the hearts of others."

In this vast universe, we are each bestowed with a limited time to leave our mark upon the world. As mortal beings, we strive not only to lead meaningful lives but also to create a lasting impact that will transcend our own fleeting presence. Yet, the pursuit of a legacy is not merely an exercise in vanity or a desire for immortality. It is an endeavor that springs from the depths of our souls, a profound yearning to etch our essence into the hearts of others and shape the course of future generations.

We will unravel the profound truth that a legacy is not forged by the number of accolades we accumulate or the monuments we build but rather by the impact we have on the lives of those we encounter.

Imagine for a moment the great figures who have left indelible imprints on history. Their names are etched upon the pages of countless textbooks, their stories whispered through generations. But their true legacy lies not in the chiseled stone or the fading ink but in the values they espoused, the ideas they championed, and the love they imparted. Like a gentle breeze, their influence continues to stir countless individuals' hearts and minds, shaping the tapestry of our collective consciousness.

Through the lens of this perspective, we will explore the profound power of authenticity, compassion, and purpose in leaving behind a legacy that endures. We will discover that a true legacy is not limited to the realms of fame or grandeur but can be woven into the very fabric of our daily lives, threading through the simplest of actions and the humblest of gestures.

As I write this book, I yearn to leave behind a little piece of myself that encapsulates the essence of who I am and what I believe in. It is a testament to my existence, a legacy that I hope will resonate with future generations, especially my beloved family.

This book is not just for them, though. It is a beacon of hope, a source of inspiration for anyone who dares to delve into its pages. Through the chapters of my life, I invite others to witness the transformational power of determination and perseverance. By sharing my story, my triumphs, and my tribulations, I hope to ignite a spark within the hearts of those who come across this literary offering.

Life, as we all know, can be full of unexpected twists and turns. It is often said that when lemons are thrown our way, we must summon the strength to make lemonade. That saying rings true in my life, as I have encountered countless hurdles and setbacks. But let me tell you, you don't have to remain confined to the circumstances of your birth. Life is a canvas awaiting your artistic touch, a symphony longing for your melodious notes. It is in your hands to shape it, mold it, and bring forth the beauty that lies dormant within.

When we first enter this world, we might believe that this is it — the culmination of our existence. But oh, how wrong we are! Life is an ever-unfolding tapestry, a continuous journey of self-discovery and growth. And that, my friends, is the essence of my legacy, the message I wish to impart to all those who turn the pages of this book. No matter where you start, no matter the adversities you face, you have the power to transcend your circumstances and create a life that reflects your dreams.

In today's world, dysfunction seems to be an unwelcome companion for many. Yet, I assure you, it is not a life sentence. Born into a dysfunctional family, I know firsthand the challenges it can bring. But, at the same time, you must remember that your past does not define you. You have within you the strength to rise above, to break free from the chains that bind you. And if my journey serves as proof, then I wholeheartedly believe that anyone can do it.

From the dawn of time, since the days of Adam and Eve, humanity has grappled with its own imperfections and struggles. We are all born into a great life, with unique stories interwoven into its fabric. And as I add my thread to this ever-evolving narrative, I hope to inspire others to embrace their own stories to recognize that their journey is both valid and significant.

You know, there's a story that has echoed through the ages — Cain killed Abel. It's a tale of dysfunction, of jealousy, and of tragic end. And yet, as I reflect on my own journey, I can't help but draw parallels to that ancient narrative. But here's the thing, I didn't let the circumstances of my birth define me. I emerged from the shadows with determination, resilience, and an unyielding belief that anything was possible if I just applied myself.

As I look back now, my only regret is that I didn't dare to dream bigger. I had settled for the comforts of the attainable when I should have been reaching for the stars. But even with that regret, I can't deny the myriad of accomplishments that have shaped my path. If you've read my story, you know how it all began, and you have an inkling of where I was headed. But let me tell you, my journey was about more than just me.

It wasn't about the singular "I" or "me" but rather about the transformation that occurred within and around me. I expanded my environment, broadened my horizons, and embraced the notion that if I could conceive it, I could achieve it.

You see, it wasn't just my accomplishments that changed everything; it was the profound encounter with something greater than myself. I may not have included every detail in the pages of my book, for some things are too sacred, too personal to be fully expressed in mere words. But what I can tell you is that the Lord Jesus Christ found me.

In that divine intersection of grace and purpose, everything shifted. It was as if the universe conspired to guide me toward a higher calling, an elevated plane of existence. The moment I recognized the presence of something greater than myself, my life took on a new meaning. The boundaries that once constrained me faded away, replaced by limitless possibilities and a profound sense of purpose.

My accomplishments became more than mere accolades; they became stepping stones on a journey of self-discovery and divine alignment. The path ahead may not be without its challenges, but with the Lord by my side, I am fortified with unwavering faith and an unquenchable thirst for greatness.

Everything changed. It was a defining moment in my life, one that would leave a lasting legacy of who I am and what I stood for. It may not be as iconic as the tale of Ms. Jane Pittman, but it is a legacy nonetheless. It's a testament that others can look back on and say, "If she can do it, so can I." My accomplishments, though diverse, have shaped me into the person I am today.

Amongst all my triumphs, one stands out prominently — obtaining a college degree. It was a monumental achievement, not just for me but for my entire family. As the first member to venture into the realm of higher education, I felt a weighty responsibility on my shoulders. But it didn't inflate my ego, contrary to what some may have thought. Instead, it set me on a different trajectory, pushing me to strive for greatness.

However, the moment I walked across the stage to receive my college diploma, I felt a surge of overwhelming pride. Graduating Magna Cum Laude with honors was beyond anything I could have imagined. Doubt had whispered in my ear, questioning my abilities, but I had silenced it with my resolute determination. The world seemed to lay at my feet, brimming with infinite possibilities. That achievement fueled my confidence and propelled me forward.

But the successes didn't stop there. Another noteworthy accomplishment was passing the Certified Public Accountant (CPA) exam on my first attempt. It was a feat that demanded countless hours of rigorous preparation and unwavering focus. When I received the news of my success, I felt an exhilaration that surpassed any other triumph. The magnitude of what I had achieved resonated deeply within me. It was a testament to my dedication, perseverance, and intellectual prowess.

Above all, there was a divine intervention that changed the course of my life. The Lord found me and transformed me completely, leaving an indelible mark on my soul. This spiritual awakening was the foundation upon which all my subsequent accomplishments would rest.

Through my unique accomplishments, I have fostered resilience and ambition, each milestone serving as a reminder of the incredible heights I could attain when I dedicate myself to a goal. These achievements stand as beacons of inspiration, demonstrating to others that dreams can be transformed into reality through unwavering determination. As I contemplate these triumphs, I recognize that they are more than just accolades; they have molded my character and propelled me toward grander aspirations. They have imbued me with the unwavering conviction that, with faith, diligent effort, and an unwavering pursuit of excellence, all things are within my grasp.

So, I embrace my legacy, not with conceit, but with a sense of responsibility. I am driven to create a narrative that inspires others to chase their dreams fearlessly. Because I know firsthand the transformative power of determination and the profound impact it can have on one's life. I am a testament to the fact that change is possible, that barriers can be broken, and that legacies can be forged. And I hope that my journey will encourage others to embark on their own path of self-discovery and achievement, for it is through their triumphs that the world becomes a brighter, more promising place.

Some might argue that getting married and having a child should be considered major accomplishments, but for me, it didn't pan out as I had hoped. It felt like a failure; I stumbled along the way. But there is something else, another milestone that I hold dear to my heart. It was the pinnacle of my professional life — a vibrant, fulfilling career. To have had the privilege of pursuing my passions and witnessing the fruits of my labor is truly remarkable. It may not have always been smooth sailing, but that only made the triumphs more meaningful. When I think about it, I can't help but feel a twinge of envy from those who have yet to experience the joy of a fulfilling career.

As I reflect on it now, I realize that none of it would have been possible without the support of God Almighty by my side.

And then there is this book — a testament to my dedication and perseverance. I had been talking about writing it for three decades, a dream that I nurtured deep within my soul. I always knew that one day, this book would be born. And now, as I hold the finished product in my hands, I am overcome with a sense of accomplishment unlike anything I have ever felt before.

These three achievements — the creation of life, a fulfilling career, and the completion of this book — stand tall as the pillars of my existence. They are the embodiment of my dreams, my hopes, and my determination.

So as I continue my journey, I carry these accomplishments as badges of honor, reminders of the hurdles I have overcome and the resilience that resides within me. They serve as a testament to the power of faith, perseverance, and unwavering belief. And as I set my sights on new horizons, I know that with the same unwavering spirit, I can continue to achieve great things, making a lasting impact in the world around me.

As I sat there, lost in my own thoughts, I couldn't help but reflect on the path I had taken in life. It was a quiet moment of introspection, a pause amidst the chaos of everyday existence. The question echoed in my mind: *what next, Lord?* It was as if a whisper from the heavens reached my soul, gently reminding me of something I had been avoiding that needed to be done. The voice spoke of my book. Ah, yes, the book I had been evading, hoping to escape its demanding embrace. Yet, deep down, I knew it was time to face the words that had long yearned to be written. It was an arduous task, one I could have easily brushed aside, but destiny had a different plan for me. There was a story within me that demanded to be shared with the world.

In the depths of my being, I felt the presence of the Lord, guiding me through life's labyrinthine passages. Each day was a step forward, an opportunity to grow in grace and wisdom. Without His divine intervention, my legacy would be empty, a hollow shell devoid of purpose. He had been my anchor, the steadfast source of strength during the darkest hours.

My journey hadn't been without sacrifice. I had traversed treacherous terrain, making choices that had consequences, even causing ripples in the lives of those closest to me. The weight of those sacrifices was not lost on me. Yet, in my heart, I believed that they would ultimately find their own path to healing and happiness.

But life has a way of teaching us valuable lessons. I have learned through trials and tribulations, and that learning has become my legacy. It is not defined by a title or a corner office but by the transformation within me. I am actively striving to become a better person and to embody love, generosity, and gratitude.

Chapter Eleven — Today and Tomorrow

"If today is like a sour apple, tomorrow it may be a flower in bloom, be patient and outlive the pain of today, for tomorrow is a new day."

— **Anonymous**

Within the pages of this captivating book lies a profound and affirmative message that resonates with the depths of your soul: you have the power to overcome any obstacles and achieve greatness. It matters not where you began your journey or the circumstances surrounding you. Whether you were born into a picture-perfect Brady Bunch-like family or one filled with turmoil and dysfunction, your potential remains untethered, ready to be unleashed.

It is crucial to understand that your past does not define you. The message reverberating through these words is clear. You can triumph over adversity and create a life that surpasses your wildest dreams. Every hurdle you encounter, every challenge you face, can be overcome. This book is a beacon of hope, reminding you that the sky's the limit when you embrace your inner strength and determination.

Allow this message to seep into your very being: Nothing can stand in your way when you are driven to succeed. All it takes is a willingness to work hard and a burning desire to make a difference. With dedication and perseverance, you possess the ability to manifest the aspirations that dance within your mind.

Let it be known, without a shadow of a doubt, that the power to shape your future lies within you. The resounding refrain throughout these pages is simple yet potent. It does not matter who you are, where you come from, or the hand life has dealt you. You hold the key to your destiny. Harness the strength of your resolve and seize the opportunities that await.

Believe in yourself, for you are capable of astonishing achievements. Every breath you take is evidence of your untapped potential. As you embark on this transformative journey, remember that the message of this book echoes through every chapter: You can conquer any challenge, break free from the constraints that hold you back, and create a life that surpasses your expectations.

It takes more than just hard work and due diligence to achieve success. It requires resilience and the willingness to persevere even in the face of failure. No matter how many times you get knocked down, the key is to get back up and try again. Failure is not the end; it's merely a stepping stone to success. This important lesson is something I've learned firsthand, and it serves as the underlying message of this book.

Throughout my journey, I have witnessed countless examples of people who have defied the odds and accomplished extraordinary things. These individuals have inspired me to pen this book and share their stories. Their remarkable achievements have shown me that with determination and firm belief in oneself, there are no limits to what one can accomplish.

However, there was a specific catalyst that propelled me to embark on this writing endeavor — the notion that secrets can have a detrimental impact on our well-being. For far too long, I witnessed the toll secrecy took on my family.

In pursuit of my dreams, I distanced myself from them because their values did not align with my aspirations. But this book became an avenue for therapeutic release.

Over time, I had buried painful secrets, concealing them deep within me. They became a heavy burden that I had almost forgotten, as if they were locked away in the recesses of my mind. The true inspiration for writing this book emerged from the desire to confront those secrets and encourage my family to do the same. It was time to break the cycle of silence and open up a dialogue.

By addressing these hidden truths, we have initiated a conversation that allows us to move forward as a united front. No longer do we need to hide, evade, or run away from our past. This book serves as a catalyst for change within our family and ourselves. It signifies the beginning of healing, growth, and an opportunity to rewrite our narrative.

In sharing our experiences, we hope to inspire others to confront their own secrets and begin their journey toward healing. By bringing these hidden stories to light, we can collectively create a world where vulnerability is embraced and personal growth is fostered. Through our shared human experiences, we discover the strength to overcome adversity and thrive.

We have confronted those secrets that once burdened us, and now we can move forward with renewed strength. The weight that rested upon our shoulders has been lifted, and we are liberated with the truth now known. The darkness that surrounded us has dissipated, replaced by a radiant light that illuminates our path. It was necessary for the truth to be exposed openly rather than whispered in secrecy or drowned in intoxication. The truth has been set free, and it exists out there for all to see.

I firmly believe that I am currently in a positive and empowering position. The heavy burden of carrying all the secrets from this book is no longer attached to me like an appendage or a ball and chain. Perhaps, when I first surfaced with those secrets, it felt like an oppressive weight, hindering my progress. However, now that ball and chain have been severed, allowing me to soar freely like an eagle.

At this moment, I find myself in a genuinely good place. The release of those secrets has created space for growth and transformation. The freedom from the past's shackles has opened up new possibilities and opportunities.

With this newfound liberation, I can embrace life with a sense of lightness and enthusiasm. The weight of secrecy no longer holds me back, enabling me to pursue my dreams and aspirations with renewed purpose and joy.

I am filled with confidence and a sense of peace when it comes to financial matters. Money is no longer a source of worry for me. Similarly, I have reached a point where I am not concerned about how my actions may influence my relationships. This newfound stability has placed me in a prime position to mentor others genuinely. I now have the ability to guide and support individuals in their personal growth journeys. It is not only about sharing my past experiences but also providing insights into the possibilities of the future.

I once coined the phrase, "*When your past ceases to be a mere memory and instead becomes intertwined with your future, it presents a significant challenge.*"

I firmly believe that I have a bright and promising future ahead of me. As for where exactly I hope to be in the years to come, that vision is still unfolding for me. It is a vision that has not yet revealed itself fully. While I would like to have a clear-cut plan, the truth is that I am still in the process of discovering where my path will lead me.

I hold the strong conviction that each and every person, regardless of who they are, should strive to cultivate a relationship with the God of the universe. I have personally experienced the transformative power of this connection, and I have witnessed its impact on the lives of others. It is my deepest desire for my daughter, my grandchildren, as well as my future great-grandchildren to embrace this truth. I want them to be liberated from the bondage of this world and its systems. True freedom can only be attained by embracing the divine presence and guidance in our lives.

Lastly, To God I give all the glory, I give all the praise, and I give all the honor for this book. Amen.